SO-AIU-712

THE MILFORD SERIES
Popular Writers of Today

Volume Twenty-Three

Science Fiction Voices #1

Interviews with Science Fiction Writers Conducted by **Darrell Schweitzer**

Featuring . . .

THEODORE STURGEON ALFRED BESTER FREDERIK POHL JAMES GUNN FRITZ LEIBER HAL CLEMENT L. SPRAGUE de CAMP

R. REGINALD

THE *Borgo Press*

SAN BERNARDINO, CALIFORNIA

MCMLXXIX

For Lee Weinstein,
who introduced me to Latimer F. Jones, William Mirdath, and other eldritch characters I haven't had a chance to interview just yet.

CONTENTS

Abbreviations Code: AB=Alfred Bester; FL=Fritz Leiber; FP=Frederik Pohl; HC=Hal Clement; JEG=James Gunn; LSDC=L. Sprague de Camp; TS=Theodore Sturgeon.

National Serials Data Program Cataloging:

Science fiction voices. 1-

   (The Milford Series: Popular writers of today ; v. 23)
No subject headings or classification numbers have yet been assigned.

sn79-1396

ISBN 0-89370-133-5 (Cloth edition; $8.95)
ISBN 0-89370-233-1 (Paper edition; $2.95)

OCLC#4579150

Copyright © 1979 by Darrell Schweitzer.
Portions of the interviews in this book have appeared first in the following publications: "Theodore Sturgeon" in *Science Fiction Review* 20, February 1977. Copyright © 1977 by Richard E. Geis; "Alfred Bester" in *Amazing Science Fiction*, June 1976. Copyright © 1976 by Ultimate Publishing Co., Inc.; "Frederik Pohl" in *Changes*, April 1975. Copyright © 1975 by Changes Publications; "James Gunn" in *The Drummer*, October 22, 1974. Copyright © 1974 by Tixeon, Inc.; "Fritz Leiber" in *Amazing Science Fiction*, September 1976. Copyright © 1976 by Ultimate Publishing Co., Inc.; "Hal Clement" in *Amazing Science Fiction*, March 1977. Copyright © 1977 by Ultimate Publishing Co., Inc.; "L. Sprague de Camp" in *Squonk*, Summer 1979. Copyright © 1979 by Fred Ramsey & Bill Spengler. All rights reserved. No part of this book may be reproduced in any form without the expressed written consent of the publisher. Published by arrangement with the author. Printed in the United States of America by Griffin Printing & Lithograph Co., Glendale, CA.

Produced, designed, and published by R. Reginald, The Borgo Press, P. O. Box 2845, San Bernardino, CA 92406, USA. Composition by Mary Burgess. Cover design by Judy Cloyd Graphic Design. Cloth binding by California Zip Bindery, San Bernardino, CA.

809. 3876
S4165

First Edition———October, 1979

LW 205963

MOUNT UNION COLLEGE
LIBRARY

INTRODUCTION: CONVERSATIONS IN PRINT

Even if you attend conventions regularly, it isn't possible for you to meet and talk with all your favorite SF authors. Hopefully the books in this series will prove to be an acceptable substitute. A good interview is an interesting conversation which just happens to be recorded; more than that, it is a very one-sided conversation. The interviewee is the one the readers are interested in; therefore, the interviewer does as little of the talking as possible. I read interviews to find out how various writers perceive their work, their position in the field, and the world in general. I want the author to open up, to speak his mind freely, so he comes across on the printed page as a personality. This is why I have always favored the question and answer format over the paraphrase and profile—if you've read one of the latter, you've read them all, and learned little more than could be had from an elaborate dustjacket squib or an entry in one of the encyclopedias of the field. But the conversational interview can be infinitely varied. Comparing my own interviews with others of the same authors, I find they aren't the same, which I hold to be a good thing. Taken together, such interviews tell us what the person is presently thinking. Over a period of time, they are of definite historical value. There is a lot of raw research data in author interviews. I'm sure contemporary scholars in the field would be endlessly grateful if someone could go back in a time machine and interview H. P. Lovecraft, Olaf Stapledon, Ray Cummings, or whoever, or pick a major pioneer of the form, say, Jack Williamson, and interview him every ten years from 1928 on to chart the development of his career, and with it the history of science fiction. Well we can't do that, but we can preserve these talks with writers of our own time, and flesh out their bylines for readers of today. I hope you think it's worth the trouble.

Darrell Schweitzer
Strafford, PA

April 18, 1979

MONTANA COLLEGE
LIBRARY

THEODORE STURGEON

Note: This is the first interview I've ever done that doesn't begin with a question. As I was setting up the tape recorder Ted was telling me about his recent travels, and he said, "You might as well get this too," and I started recording. I think it was worth it and trust you will too.

TS: For a guy who habitually hides under a rock, has an unlisted telephone, and begs people not to record his address, I busted loose very suddenly.

I was a week in Mexico City. I did two conventions in San Diego, and one in Oakland, and one in Los Angeles, and then I went east and I was in Boston, New York, Tampa, Atlanta, and I went back to Los Angeles and I did another convention. I didn't get home for three days; I went straight from the airplane to the convention hotel. And then I kind of accidentally went to Europe last May, the end of May.

A man called me up and said would I come to his convention in Metz. I said, "Where's Metz? Where are you calling from?" He said "France," and I almost fell off my chair. And after a fascinating hassle in getting a passport, which wound up finally in his calling the American ambassador in Paris, who cabled Washington, who telegraphed Los Angeles, who called me and said "How soon can you get down here?" And I found myself on a plane going to Europe for the very first time. I went to this convention in Metz and John Brunner was there and he was guest-of-honor the following week in Ferrara. He had his car with him and he said, "Why don't you come with me?" So I did, and we drove all the way down through France, and across Switzerland, and across Italy to the sea and back to Ferrara.

Having been so far into Europe I thought I ought to go see my brother who lives in Vienna, who works for the United Nations. So I hopped on a train— a train from an English movie with a corridor down one side and plush seats and mirrors and stuff in the compartments—and went to Venice, and changed trains in Venice after somebody gave me a guided tour of the city—a *fabulous* experience—and got into a *wagon-lit*, which is one of those trains with a little

4

bed in it and a little washstand and so on, and we chugged all the way across Yugoslavia and Austria, and from there back to Germany and Holland and back to the States. And it was just an incredible, heady experience. I just wonder how long this has been going on.

And after I got back to L.A., then I went to Wisonsin and did a thing there for a couple of days with associated little colleges and high schools and stuff in between, and then came the Dublin convention, and so I went to New York and fried some fish here and proceeded to Dublin; and when I was in Dublin, in pursuit of a movie producer who had made me an offer, and whom I couldn't find, I dove into France on a one-way ticket and with no other money. After a little hairy escapade or two I found him and got a binder on the agreement. The day I cashed his check I had seven francs left in my wallet. From then on everything just went beautifully. I sold seven collections in France and made this movie deal, and met a lot of movie people.

DS: What was the movie?

TS: *When You Care, When You Love*. They approached me three years ago for film rights and I told them no because this was a novelette and was part of a novel, and I wanted to finish the novel. I didn't want any screenwriter messing with my plot. Then I forgot all about the offer and all about doing the novel too. Just about four days before I left L.A. I get a letter from him asking if I would consider their funding the completion of the novel so they could get the film rights. *That* was interesting. It really was. So that's why I was chasing him. Anyway I made it and from then on everything just went beautifully.

DS: Are you going to complete the novel?

TS: Yeah, providing we can close the deal. That will be a very good thing. I have a mainstream novel going called *Godbody*, but in addition this would be a science fiction novel and the beauty of it is it's already plotted and it's one-third finished. So it won't be too much trouble to complete it.

In the meantime I have been involved for the last two years in a very complicated business of designing an overarching contract. By mismanaging my career, I seem to have acquired about fourteen publishers, and some of these contracts have expired, some of them not. Some are unfulfilled; some are fulfilled, and bit by bit I want all these properties reverted to me and put into one publishing house, a great big publishing house that has both hardcover and paperback. I don't know yet which publishing house it's going to be.

DS: You mean it's generally better to stick with one publisher?

TS: I don't know if it is, but nobody is going to last forever, and if I should pop off tomorrow my literary estate would be a great big bushel basket full of autumn leaves. Nobody would ever find anything. In addition to that, you know perfectly well you can't buy Sturgeon anywhere. I mean here I have this great big reputation, and I'm in *Who's Who* and I have all these honors and awards and so forth, and so on, but you can find me more easily and frequently in Europe and even in Japan than you can here. It's just lack of distribution and lack of management and so on. Ballantine has a new edition of *More Than Human* coming out. They're going to do *Some of Your Blood*. *Not Without Sorcery* is out. These are the three Ballantine titles. The rest of the titles have just dwindled and disappeared, and when Ballantine runs out of print they may not appear again for a long time. You just go to the science fiction section of the book shop, and where you find lots of Matheson and lots of Bradbury—well these two guys have an agent by the name of Don Congdon who designed their careers for them and did a superb job.

But as far as I'm concerned if you find any Sturgeon it may be one or two very recent titles, but that's all. It's nice that they sell as quickly as they do, but there's never stock; there's never anything in catalogue. So what I'm doing is to put at least twenty titles back into print along with half a dozen new ones. I have enough new and unanthologized stories now to make two more collections. Then of course it'll go on to British rights and foreign translations, and so on. *More Than Human* is now in seventeen languages. It is perpetually sold all over the world. That's my big one so far. *Godbody* is going to be bigger, although it's not a science fiction novel.

DS: Do you find that you have to continue to push your work, that it won't maintain itself by itself?

TS: Well, as I say, it's a matter of mismanagement. It doesn't pay so much to push your work as it does to regularize it, you see. Get with somebody who habitually does reprint and does republish.

But *More Than Human* was remaindered in hardcover within the first year, about eight-and-a-half months after it was published. It was remaindered by the hardcover publisher, not by the paperback. This kind of thing is just incredible—of course they didn't dream that that book would be as effective as it has been.

They had no way of knowing that *Sturgeon is Alive and Well* was published in hardcover and remaindered inside of a year or fourteen months or so. The paperback from Berkley was simply allowed to dwindle without being reprinted. I got a reversion on that one. But it's been a tremendous amount of correspondence and hassle and cataloging, chasing down of rights and counter-rights, and so on. A very complicated business.

In Los Angeles there's a radio commercial for a savings company which contains the immortal piece of wisdom, ''Fifty-one percent of smart is knowing what you are dumb at.''

I have lots of documentation that I'm a real bright boy. For many years I figured this has got to be the case all across the board. Of course I can handle the income tax. Of course I can handle this matter of reversing rights. I just had to get around to it, but I knew I could do it. And so, fifty-one percent of smart is knowing what you are dumb at. I have finally come to the conclusion that there are areas in which I am really stupid. I'm a real retard.

And so now I've got a New York lawyer, and I have a New York agent, and I have a guy to chase down copyrights, and I have a Hollywood agent for screen, and I have a Los Angeles business manager. This is a whole army of people, but I'm just at the position for the first time in my life of being a writer who writes. Period. That's it. A writer who writes. I've never been able to achieve that before. I've been a writer who scratches and who scrambles and does this and does that, and feeds the rabbits, and I don't want to do that anymore. It's really a pivotal point in my existence right now.

I've come from under my rock; I'm showing my face. I suppose I have the virtue of rarity. If you'd never seen a piece of coal, people would probably be carrying it around in a ring on their fingers. It's no innate quality of my own, but I have been the invisible man for a long, long time. This is no longer true. I'm flying and moving around and being seen and whatnot. This is only good.

It did me an immense amount of good to go to France and to England. I went to England for a week and did the same sort of thing. I know I did myself a lot of good. And when I came back from Europe I went to New Jersey, to a *Playboy Star Trek* convention. Then I came to New York for the second annual World Fantasy Convention, and then in two days after the convention I have a speaking engagement in Providence at a college, and then I'm going to Tucson as guest-of-honor for next weekend, and then on to San Diego before I get home.

DS: Well when do you find time to be a writer who writes amid all this?

TS: When I get back to L.A. This has been an incredible trip, marvelous, exciting, and very rewarding.

DS: What do you consider to be the most important value in writing?

TS: Communication. At the convention last week in Great Woods, New Jersey, there was a very interesting panel in which the qualities of *Star Trek* and *Space: 1999* came up.

What filtered out of that discussion was a very interesting thing indeed. Gene Roddenberry personally, himself, has certain things that he really and truly believes in. He believes in democracy. He believes in the equality of women. He believes in the equality of the races. He genuinely and truly believes in those things, and *Star Trek* continually exemplified those things. The statement made by almost every single episode of *Star Trek* was somewhere in these areas. He also believes in compassionate treatment of people. In spite of the militaristic setup there was always that element of compassion.

Space: 1999 apparently believes in nothing except selling their product. I don't mean selling dog food in the commercial breaks; I mean selling the product called *Space: 1999*, and that's the qualitative difference between those two shows—in spite of the fact that since *Star Trek* went off the air the state of the art has increased tremendously. The visual effects are like nothing else I have ever seen, but as far as the statements that the stories make, there is nobody involved in that outfit who believes in anything, apparently.

Certainly none of these qualities. Hokey as they may seem to be they are not hokey. They're really things Gene believed in.

DS: Possibly the *Space: 1999* people have no one who has any ability to tell a story.

TS: Well, there are a lot of ironic and cynical remarks made about that. One person said that they spent so much money on special effects they had nothing left for writers. Somebody got even more catty and said that all the writing budget went into the purchase of Novacaine for Barbara Bain's face cream.

DS: Well, remember that these are the same people who made *Fireball XL5*. Somebody else said that now after spending all this time making puppets behave like people, they've turned to making people behave like puppets.

TS: You know, that same remark was made there. Very good. That's a very sound remark. It's spooky; it really is. But I really think, Darrell, that it comes down to that quality of believing in something.

Now you see what's the most important thing a writer can do—to write good, communicative, well-cadenced, and well-textured prose. Underlying that is to believe in something, to really and truly have convictions. Not the editor's convictions, or what you think the buying public's convictions are—television operates on that basis: what the people will buy and then give it to them—but the idea of believing in something. I think any writer who really and truly believes in something will have a qualitative plus, so that even if he doesn't quite write as well as Joe Blough over there, that's the thing that will win out and capture editors and the public as well.

You know, I have spent half my life or more concerned with what it is that people believe, and chuntering those things around in my head, but more and more I come to the feeling that I'm looking for people who believe in something and I *almost* don't care what it is.

There's no sense in getting extreme about it and saying do you believe in sado-masochism or in fascism or something like that. You know perfectly well that I'm not talking about extreme situations, but more and more the world and especially the United States seems to be populated by liberal-minded people who have the ability to see both sides of a question and use that ability to cancel themselves out. They walk around as zeroes.

The world has been moved and shaken by obsessive nuts. Obsessive nuts. Nobody can say that Hannibal or Atilla the Hun or Karl Marx or Jesus of Nazareth or the Buddha were even-minded people who saw both sides of the question. Winston Churchill, Franklin D. Roosevelt—they weren't; they were obsessive nuts, and they moved and shook the earth because of it. They were people who believed in something, whether it was a good something or a bad something. They were effective human beings. Napoleon and so on.

I despair at ineffective human beings, and we seem to be breeding them in hundred thousand lots, and that's a shame. So I'm beginning to be impressed more and more by people who believe in something. I just don't care what it is.

DS: Isn't there a danger they will believe in something with no regard to the truth?

TS: Well, the truth is a fairly mutable thing anyway. Part of the truth is as dangerous as a lie. The whole truth sometimes gives a totally different aspect. I don't know if truth-telling as such is really part of what I'm saying. In the long run people who produce a large structure that's based on a lie will see it collapse. It may take a while, but it does, as witness Watergate. The government was a very effective machine there for a while based on lies but ultimately it fell apart. The glue wouldn't hold. So coming down to truth and ethical rightness and the karmic rightness and so on, you build stronger structures and they are more enduring than those which are based on half truths or lies. I can't say it often enough. It comes down to matters of conviction, or the ability to believe in something and have your work exemplify that which you believe in.

DS: When you started, were your beliefs already set, or did you come to them as you went along?

TS: No. Beliefs change and grow and evolve. I think early in my life I believed in a laminated society. There were decent good people and there was the great unwashed. A very snobbish kind of idea, which I derived from my English forebears, who have always lived in a laminated society. An awful lot of that rubbed off on me, and it took me quite a while to understand that the good people come from everywhere and the bad people come from everywhere too, and that there's no category of human beings, rich or well-educated or a good family or any of these things, which guarantees their being good people. It just doesn't. You produce scoundrels and whatnot from anywhere up and down the social scale. Some of my very earliest work reflected that. Some of the things I chuntered around with before I started to write seriously. There were more stories which exemplified that kind of belief, that a well-bred kind of person would find ultimately a well-bred girl to marry, no matter where she was, and God's in his heaven and all's right with the world as long as those two can get together, being well-bred people and not of the great unwashed. This is ludicrous, of course, and these beliefs have changed very drastically. So has my politics. So has my aesthetic. It's perpetually growing and changing. I hope it always will. I never want to be locked into any ritual or any hierarchical belief. That to me is a kind of death.

DS: What's the ability to believe in something and a locked hierarchical belief?

TS: I'm not talking about blind faith. The symbol that I've adopted is the letter 'Q' with an arrow through it, which means ask the next question. The very nature of faith, the very nature of the hierarchical attitude and of ritualistics is that you do accept on faith and you do not ask the next question. *Credo*, the Latin word which means "I believe" is usually followed by a great many things which are axiomatically taken on faith. I can't do that. I have tried. I've earnestly tried to, incidentally.

My first wife was a Roman Catholic and in all sincerity I went to a priest to take instruction and become a Catholic myself as a wedding present for my wife, especially when I found out that I couldn't be married in the church. I had to be married in the parish house because I wasn't clean enough to be in the sanctuary. I was a little grubby for being that kind of gentile, or whatever.

I made a truly honest, far-out effort to take instruction, to buy the whole thing and be able to say with a clear conscience that I had converted. I couldn't cut it. I had to ask the next question.

The poor guy who was giving me instruction felt persecuted and I began to get answers like, when I questioned the Inquisition, "The Catholic Church of today cannot be held responsible for the previous actions of its renegade bishops." This I felt was the great copout of all time. I couldn't handle it. I finally had to tell him "Thanks, but no thanks." I knew he'd worked hard, and God knows I did, but I couldn't do it.

DS: Then what do you mean by belief? It seems there you came to non-belief?

TS: No, I came to a very powerful structure of belief; I found that the only force in nature which is immutable, which says stop, which says Thousand Year Reich, is the human politic in the broad sense of the word politic. That is the human thought and the human structure and human society, titles, designs, utopias, and so on. They all call for a cessation, the permanent monument, the pyramid, that which is totally secure and totally stable, and so on. Evey other force in the universe is mutable. Everything changes. The planets move. The stars move. The galaxies move. Life itself is a continual process of change and growth. Diamonds are not forever. Nothing is forever, and the firmness of my belief lies in the existence of process, or cause and effect and actual process. This is not non-belief at all. This is a religious idea, literally, in the truest sense of the word.

I think you can have guidance as far as worshipping is concerned, but I feel that worship is most potent and most cogent when it's direct.

There's a condition known as Theolepsy, which means seized of God. It's exemplified in a number of ways. For example, people speaking in tongues and going into religious ecstacies, writhing around on the floor and so on. Most organized churches look down on this kind of thing because it's direct worship, and it bypasses the secular organization called the church. The church can never make a buck out of theolepsy. It has to be done through channels.

DS: You mentioned earlier your changing beliefs in aesthetics. Where did you start and where have you come to?

TS: I have just completed two semesters teaching at UCLA, not teaching non-writers to write—that can be done elsewhere—but teaching good writers to write better. I have found that it's possible to identify and define those usually unidentifiable and indefinable qualities of really good writing: texture, cadence, and atmosphere. I have found out what they are and I have found out how to teach them, and I have been very successful in being able to do that. My own aesthetics is a greater appreciation of words, and of the texture and cadence and atmosphere involved in words, and how to achieve these things.

I don't think I want to go into it now because, as I say, it's a whole course, but it can be defined and it can be taught, and it's my particular pleasure to be able to do that.

As far as my own aesthetic is concerned, it's a perpetual learning process. You learn more and more things that you can do with words, and more and more ways to do them. It's lovely to know how you get these effects. Occasionally, you do a piece of writing and it may be tremendously effective in one way or another, but you don't know how the hell you did it. It's nice to know how the hell you did it.

DS: To what degree can writing be intuitive, and to what degree can it be deliberate?

TS: Maybe sometimes its nascence is intuitive; it comes out of somewhere in your head; intuitively, you do something right; but then when you analyze what you've done and you find out how you did it, you find it's possible to transmit it, to tell somebody else how to do it, which is a profound pleasure when it comes out right.

DS: How important is the *sound* of prose? It is important?

TS: It is in some respects. I sometimes advise my students to write aloud. It's got nothing to do with reading aloud. It has to do with an inner voice, an inner aural quality. It is difficult for me to write down on a piece of paper two successive "ST" sounds, like in "the first stage," because that's difficult to say. Somehow or other, I like Hamlet's advice to the actors when he said the words must flow trippingly on the tongue. I like them to flow trippingly on the paper the same way. I'm offended by knobby or abrasive prose. There are also ways to change the texture of what you're writing, in a way as if the top half of the page is printed on silk and suddenly it's printed on burlap, and there's a change which is abrupt and almost shocking. You may have seen that done and then tried to analyze it and wondered how on earth the guy was able to do it. Sometimes the writer doesn't know how he does it. It's just his own approach. His mood changes very abruptly, or he goes away from the typewriter and comes back feeling very differently about the whole situation, or in a new scene feeling the sun was shining and it was a warm afternoon down to the third paragraph, but as he starts the fourth the wind is howling and it's cold.

I'm using these things analogically, not actually: his whole approach is different and he dresses differently and his body relaxes differently and he tightens up because it's cold, or whatever. You don't talk that way, you don't think that way, you don't sound that way when the environment changes abruptly.

There are some writers who are capable of expressing that, not in describing the situation, but in the way they write, in the way the words fall.

DS: It seems to me that with the aural values, and the amount of lyricism possible in prose, poetry and prose are not that far apart. Would you agree?

TS: Oh yes, absolutely. My adherence to science fiction is the same as my attitude toward poetry—they're the only two forms of literary expression which have no limits whatever. None. Inner space and outer space, distance and time, past time, future time. There are no limits. You can go absolutely anywhere in poetry, and you can go absolutely anywhere in science fiction. This is its tremendous appeal to me.

Further than that, my own definition of science fiction derives from the etymology of the word science, which in spite of what the dictionary tells you does not basically mean the discovery and arrangement and retrieval of knowledge. It derives from the Latin word *scientia*, which means nothing but knowledge.

To me science fiction is knowledge fiction. The operating rule is that if you take the science aspect out of the story, the knowledge aspect, and the story then collapses, that was science fiction. If you take the knowledge aspect out of the story and the narrative remains, then that's the cowboy story that was told on Mars instead of in Arizona, and it's not science fiction. It's the same essentiality that exists as far as specific sex is concerned in a story. If you can remove the essential sex and still have the story, then it wasn't essential and it shouldn't have been in there, but if the entire narrative collapses once you remove that scene, then it was necessary and it should not be removed, no matter how explicit.

DS: Have you ever had problems with editors over this?

TS: No. I've never run up against that. Once in one of my works—I think I'd rather not say which one, and let the reader guess—an editor did suggest that I remove a word which was the key to the whole book—it was a novel—purely because it was structurally better without it. And I agreed with him, but it was nothing he insisted on.

He pointed out that the book would be stronger and better and more of an experience to the reader if he figured this thing out for himself. It was crucial to the entire book. That was the only time that anyone has come near censoring me for anything I've done.

Now there have been times when there have been attempts at pre-censorship. I'll give you two recent examples.

Roger Elwood let it be known that he did not want to ever publish a story in which the devil wins. Roger has his own particular religious bias. He is welcome to it, but as long as he has that attitude, I'm not writing for Roger Elwood. Not that I would ever think of writing a story in which the devil wins. That is not the point. I just don't want to be told that I can't do it.

Another example is the letter that was sent to writers by George Scithers for *Isaac Asimov's Science Fiction Magazine*, in which he said that the magazine would have no part of any four-letter words or sex scenes.

I can't remember a single story that I've ever written that had a backyard word in it. Maybe I have, but I don't think so, and I don't see any reason why I ever should, but by God don't tell me up front that I can't. I find this very offensive. So I'm not writing for that magazine either.

This is something I feel very strongly about. I feel that quality will win. I feel that the good will always drive out the bad as far as literature is concerned. I think if the effort is made toward quality the quality stuff will outlive the rest.

I know that's probably naive of me, and maybe there are examples of where that doesn't work, but always remember that the classics are good commercial properties, purely by their very nature. They are things that thousands and thousands of people have known and liked, and they are the standards by which other things are measured.

Things are either like the classics or brand new and original and not like the classics. That's not to say that things which are widely popular are classics. It's not reversable. I say the classics are good commercial properties. I did not say good commercial properties are classics. If that were the case *Valley of the Dolls* would be a classic like Shakespeare, which obviously it isn't. But you notice that Shakespeare endures and nobody is reading *Valley of the Dolls* right now.

DS: You know, *Valley of the Dolls* will probably not be a sound commercial property in ten years.

TS: Yes, you're quite right. You're absolutely right.

DS: But it seems we've had a case with Elwood in science fiction of bad driving out the good. By flooding the market with large numbers of bad original anthologies, he's got a lot of readers who simply will not read an original anthology, and he has turned the whole market into a wasteland. So this would be the reverse of what you say.

TS: Yes, but it's a temporary situation. I say quality will win out. I don't say it wins out immediately, or that it can combat these floods of bad that come in from time to time, but in the long run over the decades and over the centuries quality will win out and quality stands.

DS: Why wouldn't you write a story in which the devil wins?

TS: I probably would if that occurred to me. What offends me is being told up front not to. I might write such a story for someone else. If Elwood or any other editor holds that in his particular credo, he does not want that done in his work, then I give him that privilege. He just won't get it from me. I never would do that if it's going to offend him, but this comes not so much from a subservience to his wishes as an absolute indignation at being told what I can and cannot say.

DS: In the early days of your career didn't you have problems trying to slip things past Kay Tarrant and people like her?

TS: Well, that was in a very light-hearted way. George O. Smith once put a thing in a story about how somebody invented a ball-bearing mousetrap, which was a tomcat, and it got into the magazine. It went right over Katie Tarrant's head. She just didn't have the vibes to pick that one up. But Campbell hugely enjoyed the fact that it got into print, and so did the readers. I don't know if Katie was ever aware of that or not. But that was never a matter of profound importance.

She was much more interested in the word itself than anything the word might possibly mean. This is why in "Killdozer" you'll find bulldozer operators out in the field saying, "I don't give a care." That's Katie at work.

DS: She rewrote that line?

TS: It was "I don't give a damn." That's the kind of thing she was zeroing in on, but you can see that it's not a matter of great importance.

DS: Well, it can make your dialog sound silly.

TS: Yeah, it can, but that's a minor point. This story was strong enough to carry itself. Horace Gold used to change lines at *Galaxy*. In his case it was more of an aesthetic matter than one of meaning. He did tangle with his authors from time to time. He never wanted to censor. In some ways Horace was like—I must say he was one of the finest editors who ever lived—but from time to time he was a little like the proverbial Hollywood producer who is always going to improve everything by changing it. It almost didn't matter what it was he changed as long as he changed it. Horace had his own ideas. He had a good rationale—good for him. I can give a perfect example. Do you remember Pangborn's story, "Angel's Egg"?

DS: Yes.

TS: Well, he had a perfectly beautiful line. It made me catch my breath it was so beautiful. When the angel was growing up she learned to fly. She was still a little bit of a thing, about eight inches tall, and she flew high up in the sky. If she touched the hero's forehead she could convey thoughts very freely, but when she wasn't touching him all she could do was send emanations: feeling good, feeling frightened. Here she was high up in the sky when he saw to his horror that there was a Cooper's hawk zeroing in on her, and he was terrified as the two spots merged, the bright spot of the angel and the dark spot of the Cooper's hawk, and at that moment, aware of his fear for her, she sent emanations of safety and of joy that it was all right. Don't worry. And Pangborn wrote that he knew then that she was riding on the hawk's head "with her speaking hands on his terrible head." I loved that line. It was absolutely beautiful. But when the story came out in the magazine that line was changed to read: "with her telepathic hands on his predatory head." I just blew my top. I remember I called Horace immediately and the phone was busy, and it turned out the reason the phone was busy was that Groff Conklin was calling him up too, and was complaining bitterly about the same thing.

DS: Did it ever get changed back?

TS: I don't think so. I think it still exists in Horace's form. No, I have a feeling that it was changed back when the story was anthologized. [Note: After doing this interview, I checked. When "Angel's Egg" appeared in Damon Knight's *A Century of Science Fiction* the line was changed back--DS.] But Horace's rationale for that was that in his mind he took a very nuts and bolts concept of what "speaking hands" meant. That meant to him deaf and dumb talk, waving your hands and tapping your fingers to the palm and curling your fingers. That's speaking hands to him. As far as "his terrible head," which is a perfect use of the word and exactly what Pangborn meant, he heard in his mind people riding the subways saying, "I had a *terrible* day" and "I just saw a *terrible* movie" and "She looked just *terrible* this morning," and he regarded the word "terrible" as a cliched word, and thought that predatory was much more descriptive of the head of a Cooper's hawk. That was his rationale. The poetry of it utterly escaped him.

DS: Was he stylistically tone-deaf?

TS: I think he was in some respects. He was always more interested in matter than in manner. But you know, I owe Horace so very much. One of the most important things that ever happened to me as a writer was one time when he'd saved space for me in an upcoming issue and I had a deadline for a novelette of 20,000 words or so, and he called me up and said, "Hey, where's the novelette." And I began to cry a lot over the telephone. This was the time of the Mc-Carthy hearings. The whole country was in a grip of terror; not having been through it you just would never understand how awful that was. It was a *frightening* thing. It crept into all the corners of the houses and everybody's speech and language. Everybody started to get super-careful about what they said, what they wrote, and what they broadcast. The whole country was in a strange type of fear, some great intangible something that nobody could get hold of. A very frightening thing.

I had become aware by that time that I had a fairly high calibre typewriter, and I became alarmed by the fact that I wasn't using it for anything but what I call "literature of entertainment." I don't want to knock entertainment at all, but I felt I had the tool to do something and I didn't know what to do with it.

Horace listened to me with great care, and he said: "I'll tell you what you do, Sturgeon. You write me a story about a guy whose wife has gone away for the weekend, and he goes down to the bus station to meet her, and the bus arrives, and the whole place is full of people. He looks across the crowd and he sees his wife emerge from the exit talking to a young man who is talking earnestly back to her. And he is carrying her suitcase. She looks across the crowd, sees her husband, speaks a word to the young man, and the young man hands her her suitcase, tips his hat, and disappears into the crowd. She comes across to the husband and kisses him. Now then, Sturgeon, write me that story, and by the time you're finished the whole world will know how you feel about Joseph McCarthy.

For a moment I didn't know what the hell he was talking about, and it comes right back to what I said earlier. If a writer really and truly believes in something, if he is totally convinced, he has a conviction, and it really doesn't matter what he writes about. That conviction is going to come through.

And at that point I sat down and wrote a story called "Mr. Costello, Hero," which was as specific and as sharply-edged a portrait of Joe McCarthy as anyone has ever written. Not only the man himself and his voice and his actions and his speech, but his motivations, where he was coming from, what made him do what he did, which I had never analyzed before.

And that was the virtue of Horace Gold that quite transcended any kind of small tone-deafness that he had, or the irritating habit he had of changing words apparently sometimes just for the sake of changing them. That was something profoundly important and pivotal to me as a writer. I suppose I had always written that way, but I never realized I did. I had never realized the conscious importance of writing that way, of being a convinced human being.

DS: How did the story go over when it came out? You must have ended up getting called a Communist for it.

TS: Sure I did. I got hate mail. I got anonymous letters. But I had spoken my piece and I was proud of it.

DS: Wasn't it true at the time that science fiction was the only area of writing that wasn't censored for these reasons, where one could get away with such things?

TS: I don't know. Science fiction writers come in all hues of the political spectrum. I mean, they really run the whole gamut to absolute extremes in all directions, although I don't think too many science fiction writers go to the very far left. A good many of them to tend to drift to the right with one or two extreme examples. I don't think science fiction has ever particularly been a repository for the far left, very largely because science fiction writers by and large, even the right-wingers, tend to be also free souls. If you're a right-winger, it's a right-winger in the sense of trying to get rid of the income tax, and of fighting against the concept of a large, central government.

DS: You mean Libertarians?

TS: Libertarians essentially. As far as the left-wingers are concerned, the left-wingers more and more approach the beehive society, the adherence to the rigid rules of Marx and Engels and so on. I think science fiction writers are generally far too free in their minds to conform to this. To quote Asimov, the "What if?" syndrome, and the "If only" and the "If this goes on." These things are too important to the science fiction writer to get bound up in any particular ideology. Science fiction writers, it seems to me, if you can categorize them—by and large it's not fair to, but I believe you can—are not ideologues, although they can get drawn into specific causes. There was one writer, I forget who it is, who became absolutely obsessed by the horrors of limb transplants, and his writing for a time became an absolute crusade against the idea of limb transplants. He extrapolated it, and was afraid that people would be farmed out, and prisoners perhaps be raised to grow arms and whatnot for other people.

DS: Is this Larry Niven? He had organ banks and the like, and people smuggling them and selling them illegally and killing people in alleyways for their organs.

TS: That's right, and Fred Pohl went into that in *Gravy Planet*, as I recall. He touched on that, but it was somebody else who became truly obsessed with it for a couple of years sometime, in the early Sixties. I can't remember who it was, but there were several stories involving a total horror of this thing. Science fiction writers tend to get sometimes these rather specified obsessions and work them out in their stories, rather than fall into any established political ideology. Or religious one, either. There have been some superb religious stories in science fiction, and several anthologies of these, and they're always very interesting.

One of the most powerful explications of established religion and its various effects is Marion Zimmer Bradley's *Darkover Landfall*, in which she has a priest who gets himself involved in a tremendously orgiastic situation. It really isn't his fault, but it involves homosexual rape and murder, and a number of things like that. He is right tight in the middle of it. But actually there is a spore that drifts across at a certain season, and these people from a wrecked spaceship are trying to survive, and when this thing hits then the whole place just goes crazy. And he comes to the edge of suicide, but then realizes that as a priest this is the very worst thing he could do. He has already done so many terrible things, but this is the worst.

That is rule one. That is axiomatic. You do not kill yourself. Life is too precious among the survivors for them to commit a capital publishment on anyone. So the priest is set to burying the dead and taking care of the graves. He is a pariah. He goes off by himself. And there's a marvelous dialogue between him and a young girl who comes out. She has something to confess and there's nobody to confess it to. He no longer considers himself a priest, and there's this dialogue between them which covers the whole question of his philosophy and his theology and the feeling of established religion as it extends itself into outer space, into new planets and new cultures. A fascinating discursion. It really is, and all honor to Marion Zimmer Bradley for that.

By the way, if you'd like to see the quote of that section completely, I used it in the chapter I wrote for Reginald Bretnor's first book on science fiction, *Science Fiction: Its Meaning and Its Future*. It was a beautiful piece of writing. In that connection let me say how pleased I am at the explosive growth of women in science fiction. Women science fiction writers are just damn good writers. Not necessarily from a feeling of bias, but I am so pleased to see that happen. After all, it began with a woman, didn't it?

DS: How do you account for the fact that women writers in science fiction are still in the extreme minority, but with one or two exceptions they're all in the top rank?

TS: Yeah, that's right. Also, some of the ones who aren't in the top rank aren't because they haven't written enough top rank stuff. I think immediately of Doris Pischeria, who really ought to write more, and particularly of Josephine Saxton, who is *incredibly* good. Did you ever read a little book called *The Hieros Gamos of Sam and An Smith*? It's a strange title and a strange little book, but it's unique. There's a distinction between a unique book and an original one. Mickey Spillane writes an original. After he's done that everybody can copy it. Dashiell Hammett did. Even Hemingway in a sense did, and people can copy his style and approach. But a unique book is something that couldn't be duplicated even by the author. There's a very slim shelf in the back of my head of books I consider truly unique. *Finnley Wren* by Philip Wylie, for example. A book by Guy Endore called *Methinks the Lady*. And *The Hieros Gamos of Sam and An Smith* belongs there with these unique books. It could never be duplicated.

DS: Wasn't this one of the books that only came out as a Doubleday hardcover and never as a paperback?

TS: No, there was also a paperback. I met Josephine Saxton, by the way, a few weeks ago. I was in London, and she did me the honor of coming up from

Staffordshire to spend the afternoon with me, and I found her an absolutely fascinating woman. She's as unique as her work.

DS: Why did all these first-rate women writers suddenly arrive just now?

TS: I think they simply found out they could. You know, something peculiar happened to me with this operating principle of permission. I have a friend in Los Angeles, and when I had this telephone call asking if I would like to go to Metz, I was very excited about it. I had no knowledge at the time or any dream of going to Italy with John Brunner. But I said to her, "I'll be there for four days and I'll come right back again, and I'm really fighting with all my heart the temptation to go to Austria to see my brother, because I haven't seen him for eleven years; I'm going to be in Europe that close to him, and I'd be tempted to go, but I'm fighting off the temptation because of the work and the money, and so on."

And she said to me: "I think that's silly. Go and see your brother. *I give you permission to go and see your brother.*" We're friends, but she has no authority over me in any way. But you know, that was magic. Somebody gave me permission. It's amazing the potency of that phrase. Isn't that strange? I give you permission to go and get the catsup, or to tell that girl you love her, or whatever.

I think that in a broad sense the times, the trade, the area of science fiction has now said to women: "I give you permission to write here." And suddenly with heady acceptance of that permission they have come in and done such extraordinary work.

DS: Do you think that because they perceive things differently is the reason they write so well?

TS: I've often thought that, and I've had arguments particularly with women's lib types whenever there'd be any assertion on my part that women think differently from men. But I think it's so. John Campbell used to deny that. He would say that women were different, but denied the idea of women's intuition, the quantum leaps of understanding that women so often seem to perform. He called it "instantaneous computation." He maintained that the intervening step did exist. The fact that women could not recall the intervening step did not mean it did not exist.

But some people feel that intuition is genuinely a quantum leap. There was a German scientist, someone associated with magnetism, who said: "I already have my solution. What is troubling me is the means," which is a good description of that intuitive leap.

I think women do tend to think in quantum leaps—this is of course a by and large thing that doesn't apply to all of them, like the statement that men are taller and stronger than women on the average. There are women who are taller and stronger than some men. So I'm not trying to be categorical about it. But whatever the difference, it absolutely fascinates me. I adore women. I like to be around them. I like to watch them. I like to touch them. It just fascinates me the way women's minds work and the way they conduct themselves. I'm thoroughly interested in that and always have been. Always will be, I think.

But it's also perfectly true that they have a way of going sometimes to the absolute heart of the matter without any fooling around, and it's shocking sometimes, like a bucket of icewater in the stomach, how swiftly a woman can get into the heart of the matter when she really and truly wants to. Also, women have an ability for endurance, for acceptance, for the ability to handle a situation which is really too complex to describe. I go into this in *Venus Plus X*. So many women seem to have what I call blackout words. A woman who's capable of learning to use a double-entry bookkeeping machine, or the most complicated kind of zig-zag sewing machine, which most men, even mechanically-minded men, would be baffled by—as soon as you say the word "transmission" or the word "frequency" everything seems to go blank in their heads. They don't know what you're talking about and they don't make the effort to find out.

DS: How much of this is a social role?

TS: A good deal of it. I don't doubt that. I'm just saying I'm fascinated that the phenomenon exists.

DS: A biologist friend of mine insists there are physiological differences between the brains of men and the brains of women. Allegedly, the hemispheres specialize late in women, and the result is men have better spatial perception.

TS: I wonder how much of that has been actually verified experimentally, and how must is just straight hypothesis. It's hard to put that one together, really. One girl I know is still in her teens and was teaching math at MIT at the age of fifteen. She's super-brilliant. She's a total mathematician. I know another girl who was a professor at USC and was teaching Old English as a language in order to read *Beowulf* in the original, and was handling it with the back of her hand. She has an IQ of about 183. I don't know if any of these categories that your friend mentioned would apply to either of those girls. But there again, maybe they're just purely exceptional. I wouldn't know.

You're right about it being a matter of societal roles. At the word "transmission" a woman's mind goes blank. There's something in her which says, "This is not feminine. I will not be desirable as a woman and as a person if I show any knowledge in this area," although she's capable of doing mechanical things which are much more difficult. It's all right for her to run sewing machines in any degree of complexity. It's not all right for her to put a new transmission in a Volkswagon (which my wife, incidentally, just recently did). Women are indeed capable of these things. I guess it's a matter of what I said, permission. Somebody gives them permission to do it.

DS: Why should any individual wait for permission?

TS: I don't know. But they do.

DS: Can't somebody control society entirely by giving or withholding permission?

TS: I don't know. I could discuss that with Mr. Skinner and see. He pictures a society run by giving and withholding rewards. Never punishing, just a matter of rewards. He claims anybody can be conditioned into doing anything that way. I find that offensive. I really do.

DS: Thank you, Mr. Sturgeon.

ALFRED BESTER

DS: You state here (in the essay, "SF & the Renaissance Man" by Alfred Bester, in *The Science Fiction Novel*, edited by B. Davenport [Advent]) that the purpose of art is to entertain and/or move its audience, and that science fiction can entertain but not move. Why is that?

AB: Because most SF writers don't know enough about people to write real people with real problems, and you can't move a reader unless you write about real people with real problems. Alas, I'm sorry to knock my colleagues in the profession, but most SF writers know very little about life and very little about people, and therefore the reader finds it difficult to be moved by them. This is why SF calls to itself people who are mostly science oriented rather than drama oriented. If there were more drama, more reality of human nature in SF it would be drawing an even wider audience than it does now. As it is, it mostly draws the people who are just curious about science.

DS: Is this a limitation of the form or the people who write it?

AB: No, no, it's a limitation of the writers themselves. What I say about science fiction is also true of television, women's magazines, skin magazines, everything. The difficulty we have in the United States is that most writers—not all, but most writers—have not yet grown up. We're not adults, and that is the difficulty we have. I think for every American novel you read that you enjoy, that's real, there are at least fifty that you read a chapter or two of and then throw it down and say, "Whoever this is doesn't know what the hell he or she is talking about. These people aren't real. I'm not interested." Now this goes for SF and it goes for all forms of writing. Since we're discussing SF I'll limit it to SF, but I really don't limit it in my mind to any particular form or medium.

DS: Why do you think there are so many overgrown adolescents writing SF?

AB: Because this country is an adolescent country; our culture is an adolescent culture. Here's an example. In *TV Guide* a couple of leading TVscript-writers were beefing like crazy that TV didn't permit them to do "serous writing," which is preposterous. I know all the guys. I know what they're doing now—they're doing the same thing that we all did thirty years ago—but your average American writer gets so *serious* about writing. It means to the average American, who is rather adolescent, something which is serious must be profound, meaningful, heavy, weighty, and this is a result of a lack of maturity. There's no such thing as a sophisticated child, and yet we seem to be sophisticated children. Ken Tynan put it best when he spoke of Americans as being sophisticated illiterates. That's what we are, as writers and as readers.

DS: Why are we sophisticated illiterates?

AB: We're sophisticated because of the media. We're very hip about everything that's going on. Why are we illiterates? Because I don't think many of us received a decent education, and I don't think that if they have received a decent education it has stuck with them, point one. Point two, I don't think the average American has had much experience in life, genuine experience. We have been very sheltered. It's only in the past generation or so that the young people have—*thank God*—been pointing out to the adults "You don't know what it's all about." I have believed for a long time—it's very cynical—that this country is not going to grow up until we lose a war, until we get licked and then occupied. Then we'll grow up, but not until then. So far we've been—well they tell that old gag about the couple of guys from Boston who were on a train from New York to Boston and one of them says to the other, "Whatever happened to Jennifer?" "Oh she's living in New York." "Oh is she really? What's she doing?" "Oh I have very bad news about her. She's doing something awful." "What is she doing?" "She's a prostitute." "Oh thank God!" said the other one. "For a moment I thought you were going to say she's living on capital." We in the states have been living on capital all our lives, which is why ecology came along too late and says for God's sake, don't destroy this heritage of ours. We have been getting fat and rich destroying our heritage and now we're beginning to wake up just a little bit with the oil squeeze.

DS: Do you think it's possible to—?

AB: To grow us up? No, as I said before, the only thing that's going to do it for us is to get licked in a war, nothing else, because we're fat and lazy and don't know what the score is. If I were president of the US I would pass a law, the first law I would pass, which would require every American citizen to spend two years living abroad in Europe, China, anywhere, to learn what the score really is.

DS: Do we then find greater maturity in foreign writings?

AB: Foreign writing? Yes, indeed, yes.

DS: Even foreign SF?

AB: Oh I haven't read much foreign SF—I haven't had the opportunity to read much of it, but the little that I've read—is it more mature? In a sense, yes. I've read mostly the French writers, and they seem to have a delicious sense of humor which is of course a part of maturity. Hey—I was going to tell you the story about the elephant that robbed the jewelry store. 47th street is the big jewelry center in New York and this jeweler comes to his shop—it's a very elegant shop, selling precious stones—he comes quite early one morning to get some bookkeeping done, and he arrives just in time to see a truck back up in front of his store and an elephant gets out of the back of the truck and with its trunk it smashes the window and scoops up all the goodies and gets back into the truck and the truck drives off. They guy is absolutely flabbergasted and he calls the cops at once, of course. The police come and they start asking questions. Well, what kind of truck was it? It was a rental truck. Did you see the guy who drove it? No, no, I can't give you a description. Well was it an African elephant or an Indian elephant? What do you mean? There's a difference? Yeah, the African elephant has big ears which stick out wide on both sides of his head, and the Indian elephant has little small ears that stick close to its head. And the guy says, 'Ears, ears, ears! How could I tell? The elephant wore a stocking over its head.' [laughter]

DS: With some pretense of seriousness, I notice in this essay here, you are talking about the limitations of science fiction as a form. What do you think they are?

AB: The limitations of SF? That's a tough question. I think the main limitation of SF is that it must, *ipso facto*, be make believe. You enjoy reading make believe stories now and then, but not as a steady diet. I think that's about its only limitation. That and the fact that too many of the writers are rather childish and don't write about human beings. You see, when I write I try very hard; with, or without success I don't know; to use science as an excuse to present human beings with new problems, new conflicts, and they try and figure out how they're going to solve them, how they're going to cope with them. Sometimes they do cope; sometimes they fail. But for me science is only the excuse to hit people with novel problems. That's what I try to do. When I read SF I read it with the same thing in mind. I want to read about real people facing the problems of the future or of extrapolation. And I do read stories like that occasionally, but not as often as I would like to. Usually you find that the men who are best on extrapolation of science are weakest on characters. You find that the people who are best on character don't know enough science to write science fiction.

DS: Why did you turn to SF when you did? Back in 1939, when your first story appeared, the field was not exactly producing sublime classics of literature.

AB: For a very simple reason. Of course as a boy I fell madly in love with science fiction. I read it constantly. I took a crack at writing because I didn't know what else to do. So what kind of writing to do? The kind of writing I knew best, which would be science fiction. I was not likely to attempt a Dostoyevskian novel or a Tolstoyan novel, or even a Dickensian novel. I knew that I had no capacity for that. SF was a small enough, limited enough field and I had studied science. I had taken my degree as a matter of fact in the scientific disciplines here at the University of Pennsylvania. So I knew enough science and I knew enough of the field to take a crack at it. And I was very lucky. I had a funny experience. I was chatting with Robert Heinlein the other day—and I was interviewing him for *Publisher's Weekly*, and I said, 'Robert, how did you write your first science fiction story?' And he said, '*Thrilling Wonder* was running a contest for the best story by an amateur and they were offering this fifty dollar prize, and so I wrote this story, but it ran 7000 words, and I had heard that a magazine called *Astounding* was paying a cent a word, so I submitted it to *Astounding* first, and they bought it.' And I said to him, 'Robert you son of a bitch, I won that contest and you beat me by $20.' And of course winning the contest was purely a fluke. It was only with the help of the editors who showed me how to rewrite the story and make it tolerable—that's all it was, tolerable—and having sold one story I tried again, and again, and again. And very slowly I began to write SF, but when the big Superman explosion started I shifted over to comic books. They needed writers very badly. And then from comics I switched to radio, from radio to television, and I kept moving on all the time. That's all.

DS: How did you get back into SF?

AB: I kept going back all the time because, for example, in script writing very often the networks or the clients would not permit me to use an idea that I liked very much. They'd say, "Well you know, it's too novel for the public. They won't understand it.' Or else, 'Oh no, it would be too expensive to do. The budget can't stand it.' Now some of these ideas I left in my gimmick book, my commonplace book, but others just bugged me so I had to write them, and since they were kind of off trail I wrote them as SF which gave me a completely free hand. And so that's how I would go to SF and go away from it and go back to it.

DS: Have you ever had opportunities to do SF in the media?

AB: Oh yes, but I've always turned them down, because the producers of the shows wanted the kind of science fiction that was being written in the 1920s, and I didn't want any part of that. It was too far back for me. Yes, I've gone out to the Coast several times, and each time I would talk to the producers and they'd still be looking for the comic book character—what's his name?

DS: Flash Gordon?

AB: Yes, they're still looking for Flash Gordon. So I don't want any part of that. You have to move with the times.

DS: There have been serious attempts to do adult SF on television. They haven't been too successful.

AB: No, they haven't been too successful, and I think I know why. I think they haven't been successful for the same reason that SF films haven't been very successful. Your TV audience and your film audience are relatively inexperienced, so the best you can give them is Flash Gordon. Anything beyond that, anything mature in SF terms, is just too much for them.

DS: Do you think it's possible, with this adolescent audience and even more adolescent industry—

AB: Well, no, it's unfair as far as SF goes to call it an adolescent audience. Let's say that it's an inexperienced audience. In SF terms an unsophisticated audience, so you have to give them the simplistic kind of SF.

DS: Is it possible to get anything better?

AB: Certainly, and as soon as you educate your audience you give them better and better. Sure, but it'll take time.

DS: It is generally agreed that there is no work in SF right now which is to be considered among the greatest works of human literature. Do you think we'll ever get such a work?

AB: Well, you know, it all depends on your definition of the greatest works of literature. That's a tough one, really. You take a novel, for example, like Reade's *The Cloister and The Hearth*. That's high style, almost picaresque writing—well it's high adventure writing. Theoretically this would be the equivalent of a science fiction novel. Have there been SF novels equivalent to that? What's my answer. No. Why not? Jesus Christ, that's a rough question to answer. How about *Mary Poppins*, which is surely a classic? Certainly if it's not SF it is fantasy and delicious fantasy too. So there have been fantasies which have been classics. *The Wind In The Willows* for example. There's a great classic for you, a beast fable. *The Wind In The Willows* is marvellous. Have there been SF classics? How about *The War of the Worlds*? That's a magnificent novel, really magnificent. That's great literature. So SF can achieve it.

DS: Something that Robert Silverberg once brought up in an interview was that SF had yet to produce its Shakespeare.

AB: Well so has literature. After Shakespeare what? That s.o.b., he's the death of every writer. He's so great that you're always writing against him and losing. But we produced one Shakespeare, period, and so to ask for another is asking too much. Why not say has SF yet to produce its Dickens or its Reade or its Nancy Mitford? I don't know. How about Lewis Carroll? SF has yet to produce its Lewis Carroll. That I think is a fair comparison. These kinds of great talents only show up once every four or five generations. We have to be patient in between, that's all. Someone will come along in SF. For all we know some novel which we take for granted, we may discover if we live long enough, that in time it will become a great classic of literature. *The Space Merchants*, which I think is one of the finest SF novels ever written, may well turn out to be a classic.

DS: Do you think such a great novel will be recognized?

AB: No, of course not.

DS: Later?

Later, surely. It'll be recognized later, and it'll be a great surprise to us to find out, "What? That thing's a classic? It was just another book I read, that's all."

DS: Do you see anybody in the field right now with classic potential?

AB: Oh man, that's a tough one. You must understand, I am not knocking any writer—I absolutely refuse to do that—but the writers that I praise, that appeal to me the most, may not necessarily appeal to the world. For example, Theodore Sturgeon. I have always adored everything that Sturgeon has ever written. And if anyone is capable of producing an all time classic it certainly is Ted. Who else? Well you know I am a great, *great* admirer of Cyril Kornbluth's, and a great admirer of Henry Kuttner. Kuttner I thought was like God, and alas, alas, alas, Kuttner died, but some of his short stories are great classics. Do you remember one called "Vintage Season?" He wrote it under the name of O'Donnell. Gee, that's a great story. He had the master touch. Why am I still alive and why is he dead? It should be the other way around, because he really had it.

DS: In this essay you mention that the appeal of SF is basically that of "Arrest Fiction," meaning it's something that grabs ahold of someone—

AB: Oh yes, sure. Again I'll quote Robert Heinlein. He said, 'Look what I do. I grab you off the street, grab you by the lapels—I never let go—and I shake you.' Well, that's arrest fiction. That's what he does. I do it in a different way. I shoot bullets past their heads. But it's the same damn thing. I mean you shake them up and knock 'em as silly as you can, hopefully entertaining them while you're doing it.

DS: How do you design a story to shake the reader?

AB: Well first I have to shake myself. One example. Ben Bova had exactly the same reaction. In this novel that *Analog* was running, there came a point at which it suddenly dawned on me that I would have to kill off my favorite character, a lady. And it just came on me, slowly, but surely, Alfie you gotta kill her. The cast of characters and the balance of the story require it. It's absolutely necessary. Well, I couldn't write for a week. I just couldn't bring myself to write the death scene, because I loved her so much and she was such a part of me. And finally I got up the guts, and I killed her. And then I went into complete shock and couldn't write for a week after that. She was dead. My baby was dead. And I was delighted when Ben got the manuscript and read it and said, 'Alfie when you killed off so and so I was in complete shock. It killed me that you killed her.' I said, 'Yeah, it hit me the same way.' I have to surprise myself and astonish myself and shake myself up. And if I can do it to myself, hopefully it will have the same effect on the reader.

DS: Do you consciously use stylistic tricks to achieve this, such as the unusual typography in *The Stars My Destination*?

AB: No, that's not done for the purpose of shaking them up. It's done because of the attempt on my part to create an entire milieu, to build an entire civilization. And I find that I must, in order to do that, use visual as well as literary imagery. It's not done just for the sake of a trick. It's done because it will add some color to the particular milieu in which the story is taking place. That's all.

DS: Did you have a lot of trouble with the typesetters and proofreaders on that and on *The Demolished Man*?

AB: No, not really. No trouble at all. My editors understood what was being done and monitored the production of the books very carefully. Where I've had the most difficulty and still do is where I deliberately use bad grammar. You'll always find a copy checker who's going to clean up your grammar. You know, they did that to Ring Lardner once. It's a classic story about copy checkers. Ring Lardner of course was famous for writing stories from the standpoint of the narrator who as often as not was a dumb ballplayer or dumb prizefighter or something, who used miserable grammar, and one publishing house published one of his stories and they cleaned up all the grammar, which of course destroyed the story. They had missed the entire point. Now the same thing happened to me when I quoted a line of Ring Lardner's, "Writeing is a nag." Of course 'writing' is misspelled, and what the character was trying to say was "writing is a knack" and that's the way Lardner wrote it. And that's what I used for a piece I wrote for an English publication and dammit if the copy checkers didn't clean it up, and I had to send the copy back and say "Stet! Stet! Stet! Sic! Sic! Sic!" This is the way it is. I have this trouble all the time. As a matter of fact Diana King at *Analog* had a hell of a problem because sometimes my misspellings were deliberate and other times they were accidents. And she had to figure out whether it was deliberate or stupidity.

DS: Well, I just ran out of questions.

AB: Oh, that's all right, I'll ask a few questions. What aspect of SF do you think readers are most interested in about writers, the authors of SF?

DS: About the authors? What kind of person writes this? I think the guy who doesn't read SF often will ask where they get those crazy ideas, and the fan is probably a frustrated would-be writer himself, and he'll say, "How do they do it?" And the fan who is not a would-be writer—there are a few occasionally—might wonder what kind of person this is who is producing this.

AB: In the sense of, 'does he have a trick or secret that I can learn so I can write it too'?

DS: I don't think it works that way.

AB: I know it doesn't work that way, but do you think that they think it works that way?

DS: Oh, yes, especially if you talk to non-writers, the ones who have a very exaggerated concept of the value of a story idea. You know, 'I've got this great idea for a story—'

AB: I don't have the time, so all you have to do is write it for me.

DS: Yeah, the ones who don't realize that stories are people and images and experiences. They think it's just the idea.

AB: And as a matter of fact I've already said, and it's perfectly true, that you can take the identical idea and give it to six different writers and each will produce an entirely different story because after all the art is the man and the man is the art and you write what you are, you paint what you are, you sculpt what you are, and you compose what you are. It's unavoidable. And one of the difficulties I had with young writers was trying to explain to them as gently as possible, 'Look, write only what you know.' You haven't had much experience yet, you're only 21, so don't write about things you don't know about. Just write your experiences. You will eventually, as time passes, grow, experience more, and your horizons as a writer will enlarge. But be content with your limited horizons now and try, off duty as it were, to enlarge your experiences. Go out and have experiences. I used to tell that to Jim Blish all the time. I remember in reviewing one of Jim Blish's books, 'For God's sake, Jim, will you go out and chase ladies, gamble, rob a bank, do something. Get experience, because although your science is great your characters are completely unreal.'

DS: How important do you think everyday experiences are in writing SF? Won't they give the story a flavor which will badly date it?

AB: No. I'm going to use you. Someday I'll use you. I don't know what I'll do with you but I'll use you. I'm a packrat. My wife calls me a cesspool. Nothing goes to waste. I'll use you. I used to know a guy, an Englishman, who was a colleague of mine and we were writing the same TV show together. He was doing research on it and I was writing the script. He also wrote himself, but he didn't really believe he was creating unless he made it up out of whole cloth. He had to invent everything. And I would say, 'For Christ's sake, this character is not real. Will you use somebody you know if you need a character?' No, he had to invent everything. As a result his stories were completely unbelievable.

DS: How do you account for an imaginary world fantasy, such as *The Lord of the Rings* or the James Branch Cabell books?

AB: I hate it. Sure, I hate Cabell. When I was a kid I used to enjoy reading it only because of the little sex passages in it, and you know when you're a kid you like to read sexy stuff, but I hate Cabell. As for the *Ring* cycle, that's unique. Only it had some sensational chapters in the first novel. He had some other chapters which were incredibly dull. But I just prefer to think of the great chapters.

DS: Is this because his invention flagged or maybe because Tolkien was a dull person?

AB: I wish I knew. I don't know the guy. If I'd interviewed him I would have found out.

DS: What happens if a writer writes himself into a story and no one is interested?

AB: He shouldn't write it. He should give up writing and go and be an honest man and work in Gimbels or something. If you lose it you lose it. There's nothing you can impose on the reader. The reader owes you nothing. You owe everything to the reader, to entertain him. If you've lost it, too bad.

DS: Basically, a writer has to be an interesting person to begin with?

AB: That I don't know. Some of the most brilliant writers I've met have been very dull people in real life. Their writing it so happens can be fantastic.

DS: Maybe this is because they put everything in their writing and there's nothing left.

AB: It could be. It could easily be. I think that's the answer myself, but I couldn't swear to it. [pause] Running out of gas or out of tape?

DS: Both. You exhausted the first line of questioning so quickly—

DS: Are you editing full time now?

FP: No. I spend one day a week as SF editor of Bantam Books. I spend roughly two days a week fooling around and roughly four days a week writing.

DS: Are you writing for a living or editing for a living?

FP: Actually I am living now basically on royalties and things like that. I derive a certain income from Bantam Books, and a certain income from new writing, but all my years of toil and self-denial are paying off.

DS: How long have you been editing? What was the first thing you edited and how did you get the job?

FP: In October 1939, I went to an editor friend of mine, an editor I had been trying to sell stories to unsuccessfully, and as I had observed that it took no talent at all to be an editor and it did take some talent to be a writer I figured the thing to do was be an editor, so I asked him if he would care to hire me as an assistant, and he said, "Not on your life, but go see Rogers Terrill over at Popular Publications because he just might give you a job." And I went to see Rogers Terrill and he gave me two science fiction magazines to edit. I was 19 years old and had very little notion of what I was doing. But it was a form of on-the-job training because they didn't pay me enough to make any difference anyhow.

DS: What did you do when you first found yourself faced with a pile of manuscripts and very little idea of what you were doing?

FP: Well, I knew enough to know what SF stories I enjoyed reading, so I picked out the ones I most enjoyed, and that turned out to be about a quarter of what I needed to fill the magazine. So I went after writers I knew and people I knew who I thought had talent, and got them to write stories for me. Among them were a lot of amateurs with no discernable track record, like Cyril Kornbluth and Isaac Asimov.

DS: The magazines you edited were *Super Science* and *Astonishing*, right? Would you consider them successful?

FP: I don't think they were terribly successful. They appeared in a time when it did not make any great deal of difference whether a pulp magazine was good or not. They sold mostly by categories. If science fiction happened to be selling well that month they sold fairly well. If it wasn't, they didn't. They sold well enough to be kept going more or less intact until the paper shortages of World War II killed them off, but by that time I was in the Army and it was not my problem anymore.

DS: How well do you think they held up in comparison with the other magazines of the period? This is allegedly the "Golden Age" of science fiction that we're talking about. Did you have anything to do with making it golden?

FP: Very little. John Campbell (editor of *Astounding SF*, later retitled *Analog*) singlehandedly was responsible for the Golden Age. He introduced a great many new writers: van Vogt, Heinlein, Cleve Cartmill, Sprague de Camp, etc., and he retrained a good many older writers like Jack Williamson and Clifford Simak to do his kind of writing. And I had very little to do with that. That thing that made my magazines at all tolerable was that John had certain idiosyncrasies which kept him from buying some kinds of stories. For example, a story by Ross Rocklynne called "Into The Darkness" came to me because

John didn't have the wit to buy it. It was really a great story. Some of Heinlein's early work came to me because John didn't have the wit to buy it. I had a number of stories written for me by writers who, as I mentioned before, were not well known at the time but became well known later, such as Kornbluth and Asimov and Dick Wilson. I think I bought Ray Bradbury's first story. And all these things made the magazines I published tolerable, but they could not compete in any way for quality with John Campbell.

DS: Now the Heinlein stories were published under a pseudonym—

FP: That's because I was paying him something like a quarter of a cent a word. I bought three from Bob Heinlein. One was called "Lost Legacy" and it was a lengthy novella about a sort of Shangri-La in the California mountains where Ambrose Bierce turned up. One was a story called "Let There Be Light" and one had something to do with Easter Island but I've forgotten what. I think they have all been reprinted. I don't know for sure.

DS: After you got out of the Army and your magazines were wiped out by the paper shortage, what did you do?

FP: I had no intention of ever returning to editing. I was in the Army with the 456th Bomb Group near Foggia in Italy. I was kind of homesick, so I decided to write a novel about New York City, and in order to write a novel about New York City I thought it would be interesting to write about some sexy aspect of New York life. The most interesting thing I could think of to write about was the advertising industry, so I wrote a novel called *For Some We Loved*. I wrote the whole thing at Foggia or on Mt. Vesuvius a few months later, and when I got out of the Army, it occurred to me that there was one problem in having written a novel about advertising and that was that I didn't know anything about advertising. So I looked in the Sunday *Times*. There were three advertising jobs offered. I applied to them all, and one of them hired me, and I spent the next three years writing advertising copy for one person or another. During that time I had a summer place at Ashokan, N.Y., with a big fireplace, and I stayed up all of one night reading the manuscript of the novel I had written in Italy and as I read each page I threw it into the fire because it was absolutely abominable. There was nothing about it that was good. So at that point I had a great deal of information about advertising that I was making no use of, and it occurred to me to write an SF novel, so I wrote 20,000 words as the beginning of one. Then I showed it to Horace Gold who was the editor of *Galaxy* and he said, "Finish it and I'll buy it." And I asked Cyril Kornbluth to help me finish it and it became *The Space Merchants*.

DS: Some writers have said that when they get a writing job such as an advertising job, they get home and they can't even look at a typewriter, and it destroys them for writing creative work. Did this happen to you?

FP: I think this is often true. I find it very difficult to combine writing and editing, especially editing a magazine. When I was first editing *Astonishing* and *Super Science*, I didn't do a great deal of writing. I didn't even do a great deal of reading. About all I could stand to read were French decadents like Huysmans and Marcel Proust, and some of the Russians. So I stopped reading SF except for what I read professionally, and I stopped writing it most of the time for about three years. When I was editing *Galaxy* and *If* it was difficult for me to do any writing. The editing for Bantam doesn't seem to have that effect if only because I read so many fewer stories, maybe a dozen a month instead of four hundred.

DS: I noticed that when you were editing *If* you published three novels in collaboration with Jack Williamson, and you've done a lot of collaboration with another writer? Do you find it easier to get somebody else to do half the work, or does the book grow and you get twice as much out of it?

FP: Well, it depends on the collaborator. I've tried collaborating with, I guess, about a dozen writers and often it is agony. Lester del Rey and I wrote a novel together which had a big fat advance and won a prize and all that, but we could not afford to do it again because it was such hard work and it took us forever to write it. I'll never collaborate with Lester again. He's one of my dearest friends but it's impossible for me to work with him. With Cyril Kornbluth, collaboration was very easy because we had more or less grown up together. We had much the same view of the world; we thought in much the same terms; we wrote a little bit like each other, so we could discuss a story and then he would sit down at the typewriter and write the first four pages of it and I'd write the next four, and by and by we'd have a novel. It worked. *The Space Merchants*, *Gladiator-At-Law*, and so on were written just that way. With Jack Williamson, it's rather different, because for one thing he lives in New Mexico and I live in New Jersey, so he writes first drafts and I revise them. It's an awful lot of work for Jack and comparatively little for me and I'm terribly grateful to him for all this trouble.

DS: You seem to be writing piecemeal, four pages at a time—

FP: With Cyril, it didn't matter because it was the same process going on. Sometimes I'd stop at the end of a page and know what the next word and the end of the sentence was, but I wouldn't write it, and when I came to look at it, he'd written that sentence just as I had intended.

DS: Did you write all this at once or pass between sittings writing four pages?

FP: No, we'd keep a hot typewriter going. I'd sleep while he was typing and vice versa.

DS: Why did you leave *IF*?

FP: I left *If* and *Galaxy* because they were sold to a publisher with whom I had differences of opinion. One difference was that he thought an editor should be in the office from nine till five five days a week and I didn't believe that for a second. I just didn't want to do that. There were other reasons, too, but basically that was the main reason.

DS: When you left *If*, did you return to full time writing?

FP: When I left *If* and *Galaxy*—I consider I left *Galaxy*: *If* just happened to be there—I intended to go full time writing, but as it happened, Ballantine issued eighteen of my books in one year and paid me a bundle for it, so I had no incentive to do any writing. I think that one of the difficulties that confronts many SF writers today is that they are not starving and so they don't write as hard or as much as they would have if they had needed the money to pay off the mortgage or buy groceries.

DS: Do you think it is necessary to be starving in order to write? Aren't there compulsive writers who will write anyway?

FP: I think probably so, but I suspect that much of the best SF ever written was written by somebody who had to turn the story in the following day to get a check the day after or else his electricity would have been turned off.

DS: Then basically there's no difference between an "artistic" approach and a commerical approach?

FP: I didn't say that. You said that. I think that there is a difference between individuals. Some individuals will write the best they know how no matter what and some will write the sloppest they know how no matter what. I think that the difference is one of incentive. There are times when a writer knows that he has a story he can tell and feels that he can put it on paper in the form he likes, but if there's no particular urgency about it he's likely to go fishing that day, or he'll go to the theatre or take a trip or whatever. If there is some incentive, if he has to do it or have trouble, then he'll sit down and do it. I think that SF writers respond inversely to money. Much of the best Sf has been written for the lowest rates. I'm not sure why this is. It may have to do with some masochistic impulse, with a death wish, or with just the idiosyncrasies of the breed, but I think it's true. About 15 years ago, a team of psychologists made a study of SF writers, measured their traits against a comparable group of sculptors or something like that, and a comparable group of the population at large, and discovered that the SF writers differ from the other groups in several ways. They were somewhat more intelligent, but the thing in which they were outstandingly different was stubbornness. SF writers by and large are the stubbornnest people in the world. They will not be bribed with money.

FP: Do you ever find yourself rather upset because you have a story in you and you just haven't gotten around to writing it?

FP: No. Very rarely. It does sometimes happen that there's a story in me at the moment at which I can't write, and I've lost some stories that way, but more frequently it's that I'm sitting at the typewriter and I don't have the faintest idea what I want to do. And this is a painful situation for a writer. It happens not only when I don't have a story begun, but often it happens in the middle of a story. I'm not sure where I want to go with it, and my recipe for that is take the story out of my typewriter and put it in a filing cabinet and work on something else that I do know what I am going to do with. So I usually have up to ten projects going at one time.

DS: What sets you off on a story in the first place?

FP: Well, different things at different times. Sometimes two ideas come together in my head and they seem to have some relevance to one another and they come to suggest possibilities for development. There's a story of mine called "Day Million" which I can speak about very coherently because I just wrote an article about it for somebody. There are a lot of ingredients in "Day Million." One is the notion of people relating to other people as taped recordings of themselves so that if you want to marry someone, you don't marry the physical person, you make a tape of him or her and he or she makes a tape of you and you take the tapes away and live with each other all the time. This is a development of what's called Turing's Problem, which has to do with whether people are people or whether you can duplicate them with a computer. Other things in "Day Million" have to do with the ability to make sex changes and be what you want to be. If you don't like being a boy, you can be a girl, and so on. All these things came together in my head when I say down to write the story, but the reason I wrote the story had nothing to do with any of these things.

It had to do with the title "Day Million." I wanted to do a TV series under that title because I had liked it, so I decided I would write a story under that title, and publish it in order to protect the title, and I put the paper in the typewriter and typed the words "Day Million" and all these things I had been thinking about seemed to come together in my head as being related to the millionth day of the Christian era, which is what I was talking about.

DS: But the thing that got you thinking along these lines in the first place was hearing about them or reading about them—

FP: Well, what gets me thinking about notions for stories is the totality of life. It's what people do and what people say, what experiences I have, what goes through my head, what I read in scientific publications or in the newspapers or in books, what people have said to me about what they're doing or what they think. Some part of me stores up all these things and feeds them back to me when they make some sort of contact with each other. It doesn't always work very easily, and I suppose other writers may have a different view of what happens in their heads. As I perceive it, that's what happens in mine.

DS: When you say that you have ten things in the file cabinet, will most of these ten things ever be finished or will some of them just languish there forever?

FP: Well, there are some which just languish there forever. I have whole books which I have written that I haven't published and probably never will. There's a complete book on the Ku Klux Klan which I was not satisfied with so I bought the contract back. There's a book on the Great Depression I have about 300,000 words of notes for, and about 50,000 words of finished copy, but I don't like it so I bought the contract back on that, too. There are two SF novels which I have contracts on which I haven't finished which are seriously overdue, but I haven't solved the problem of how to write them yet so they're going to stay overdue until that happens, and probably a hundred or a hundred and fifty short story fragments, most of which I'll never finish because I didn't like them. They just seemed like a good idea that didn't work.

DS: When you don't like something, is this because you personally don't like it or because you think the readers won't like it? Do you write for yourself or for your audience?

FP: I write for the audience but the first person I have to convince that the audience will like it is me, and if I really think there is something fundementally wrong with it, if I think it fails to say what I want it to say or says it clumsily, if I'm aware of this, I won't go any further with it until I know what to do about it.

DS: Have you ever written a book that you felt clearly stated what you wanted to say and then discovered that everybody misinterpreted it?

FP: Never. It's never happened. I've published a number of stories that I've thought were pretty good that have not attracted any great attention, but I think that it's not that people misinterpreted them. I think I was wrong and they really didn't make their points. There's a story called "In The Problem Pit" which should have been a better story than it was. Something was wrong with it and I still don't know what. But it wasn't people misinterpreting it. It was a failure in the story that I haven't perceived. I don't know what it is.

DS: Have you ever tried to rewrite stories?

FP: After they're published? Arthur Clarke has done that, but I never had that sort of *chutzpah*. No, actually, once I'm finished with a story, I don't want to see it again.

DS: What would you rather do, write or edit?

FP: If I had to choose betwen one or the other, I would write and screw the editing. As a matter of fact, I intend to give up editing when my contract runs out June 30th of next year. I've had about all the fun I can have editing SF. I would not be editing for Bantam now except for some personal reasons. I got involved in an editorial project which I hated and it was stupid of me to get involved, but I was, and it left a bad taste in my mouth, so I went with Bantam to get that taste out of my mouth. So when I'm through with Bantam, I'm through with editing.

DS: Then you'll be writing even more than you are now?

FP: Not necessarily, but I'll be writing as long as I live, I imagine.

FP: You mentioned a book on the KKK and such things. Do you find yourself typed as a science ficion writer? Do publishers want to see SF and nothing else?

FP: I don't have that problem. I write what I want to write. The KKK book had a contract. It wasn't the publisher who elected not to publish it. I decided to buy the contract back because I didn't like it. I have published a lot of other books. I'm the *Encyclopaedia Britannica*'s authority on the Emperor Tiberius, and I published a book on practical politics, novels that were not SF, etc. There is no difficulty in getting this stuff published. There is only the difficulty of writing something that I like well enough to want to be published.

DS: If you ever got yourself in rough straits financially, would you publish the things you don't like?

FP: I have done it, but I hope to be exempt from that sort of pressure for the rest of my life. For one thing I have no particular reason to be in rough straits financially. As a writer all I need is a typewriter, which I already own, and some paper. My kids are pretty well grown and I have no particular need for anything, so I can probably get by on twenty-five or thirty thousand a year. [Laughter]

DS: You say SF writers react inversely to money? How high do you have to go before this happens? $100,000 a week?

FP: I think it is true that SF writers react inversely to money. There is also good evidence for it, but there comes a point when you're no longer writing for money because you've developed the built-in writer's annuity, royalties on stuff you've written five or ten or twenty years before, which after a point becomes enough to live on if you really want to, and at that point you have a totally free choice of what you do. You can do anything you damn well please, and I think most of us at that point curtail our production, but I don't think anybody really gives it up.

DS: Do you think they write better once they have achieved that, because they have more time to work on any individual story?

FP: I think it depends on the writer. There are writers I know that when they no longer need money write twice as much and twice as bad, but it's not true for everybody. There's a thing that happened a few years ago which is sort of relevant. *Time* magazine ran an article on SF and called me up because they wanted to run a side bar on famous SF writers of the past and what they're doing now. So they asked me about every famous SF writer of the past they could think of, and of the ones who were still alive, what they were doing now was writing SF. You either die, or you keep on writing SF.

POSTSCRIPT

DS: Now it's four years after the original interview, and a lot of things have happened. You've been collecting awards—a Nebula for *Man Plus* in 1977, and a Nebula, a Hugo and everything else in sight for *Gateway* in 1978. What else? Did you ever finish the two novels you were holding up on until you thought they were right?

FP: Funny you should ask; actually, they were *Man Plus* and *Gateway*. Since then I've finished a new novel, *JEM*—it was also about two years late, for the same reason, namely that I didn't want to let go of it until I was satisfied with it. And I am now working on two others, tentatively called *The Cool War* and *Beyond the Blue*, as well as a new collaboration with Jack Williamson called *Wall Around a Star* and a number of odds and ends.

DS: Are you still editing?

FP: No, I did in fact leave Bantam—three years later than I intended. Apart from an anthology now and then—especially one which is a sort of retrospective of all the things I've edited from 1939 through 1978—I don't intend ever to be an editor again. I've turned down two attractive offers, so I guess I'm serious about it.

DS: That sounds like you intend to spend more time writing?

FP: I don't really think I will—I've been writing pretty steadily all along. As far as I have any serious plan, which is not very far, I plan to continue at about the same pace in writing, plus a little teaching, lecturing and so on from time to time. What I hope to do more of, actually, is loafing. That is a high-priority item in my future time budget, and I mean to get to it real soon now.

JAMES GUNN

DS: Science fiction has suddenly gotten very respectable. How would you account for that?

JEG: Well, a lot of things have suddenly gotten very respectable. This is actually sort of a pop culture era, when a great many things which have occurred relatively without academic notice have suddenly had a great deal of interest in the academic area. One example of this which isn't often thought of is American studies, which came into the university curricula about fifteen-twenty years ago, perhaps a little longer than that in some places. But it was followed up by the popular culture movement which had a number of manifestations. There was the pop art which made art out of soupcans and other kinds of materials found around us in everyday life. There was the pop music which began to come into curricula in part through the respectability of jazz and through the recognition of other kinds of musicians. I remember Leonard Bernstein doing a television show five or six years ago in which he was praising the musicianship of the Beatles. So SF is following a general trend in which the pop lit, pop arts, are receiving attention, in part because students are interested in them, in part because people who once enjoyed them are now wanting to teach them, and to bring them into conjunction with the academic institutions, and in part because of a certain vitality within science fiction itself. Or to put it another way, a certain lack of vitality in certain aspects of mainstream literature.

DS: Do you think that putting SF in the classroom will have the same effect that putting mainstream fiction in the classroom did?

JEG: I don't think—when I talk about mainstream literature I'm talking about Hemingway and Faulkner; I'm talking about popular contemporary writers like John Updike, Philip Roth, and others. I don't think they've diminished their stature or diminished their popularity. If anything I suspect that they have enhanced those writers, that more people have read them, more people than would have if they had not been brought into the academy. If one looks back at certain other popular writers, like Shakespeare for instance, who was a popular writer of his day, the fact indeed that we still can read Shakespeare, that we can still see Shakespeare plays, is a product of the fact that he was recognized over the years as having something to say to us. And if indeed he had not been so recognized by the academy it's unlikely that today anyone would be conscious of Shakespeare.

DS: Do you think then that teachers form the literary tastes of the masses? If everybody studies science fiction in high school and college, will that vastly increase the readership for it?

JEG: I think it will. Not because of the teachers' forming popular taste; it will increase the readership of science fiction because young people who would not have found it otherwise are going to be exposed to it and they're going to enjoy it, and they're going to go on and read other things. One example I might give you is when I taught my first science fiction class at the University of Kansas, some four years ago, the college bookstore suddenly had a run on science fiction criticism. They happened to have been knowledgable about the matter, but they said, "We're selling out of those Advent books on science fiction criticism, and it must be your class that's responsible," and I'm sure it was. There was interest in not only the reading of science fiction, but they wanted some comment about it as well.

DS: You mean you didn't assign those books?

JEG: No, they just went out and got them themselves.

DS: Is the general reader interested in criticism?

JEG: Well, what is fandom but a kind of criticism? The general reader reads fan magazines, reads criticism. Well, the first thing I turn to in a science fiction magazine, long before I read the magazine itself, is its reviews. I don't know how many other people do that. Maybe it's my own particular interest, but I suspect that many people are interested in what a reviewer has to say about contemporary SF.

DS: These attitudes are certainly prevalent among the very active readers, but then fandom comprises at best ten percent. Do you think that the general reader, the average college student, is going to be interested in real science fiction scholarship?

JEG: I don't think he'll be all that interested in scholarship. Some of them will, some of them won't. It depends upon the depth of their interest. Some will read some of it and enjoy it and go on to read more. Others will be turned off by science ficiton. But at least they'll be exposed to it and have an opportunity to be turned on by it.

DS: Now when you are teaching a science fiction course, how do you go about it, what do you do in the classroom?

JEG: Well, you want to approach SF in a lot of different ways. I happen to teach it from a historical viewpoint. It's my conviction that a reader cannot really appreciate contemporary science fiction unless he knows how it got to be contemporary SF. And so I try to trace the evolution of science fiction, what made it what it is, through the study of certain historical trends, sociological, technological, and scientific influences, which eventually produced over a period of a couple of centuries what we know as science fiction.

DS: How does your being a teacher of science fiction affect you as a writer? Do you find this very compatible or does it take up writing time, or what?

JEG: Well, there's no doubt that whatever you do takes up time you could be using for writing. At the same time I should say that being a teacher gives me some freedom to write only what I'm really interested in writing, and that which I think is worth writing, rather than what might sell. There are many people who are full-time science fiction writers who turn out work not because it is particularly what they want to write, but because it is what they know they must write in order to meet the bills. Fortunately, having another kind of job, which I like very much, teaching, gives me the opportunity to be very choosy about what I want to write, and it is true as well that the academic scene provides, and in fact expects me to do this kind of work. It is part of my responsibility as a teacher of fiction writing and as a teacher of science fiction, to be creative in this area.

DS: Then if every science fiction writer had another job to support him, wouldn't the quality of the field as a whole go up?

JEG: Everybody's different; you can't generalize from one person's experience for everybody. I think for some people the discipline of full-time writing is essential. I did write full-time for a period of 4 years and if it hadn't been for certain circumstances I might be freelancing now. But for some of us, a few of us, having a compatible job like this gives us a certin advantage. Some people, I suspect maybe Phil Klass is one of them (better known by his pseudonym *William Tenn*) find all their energies going into teaching and do very little writing. Others like myself are able to adjust to these different demands and spend energies both ways. I might also say that it seems to me that perhaps teaching brings a different quality to writing as well. When one is teaching literature one becomes conscious of certain values that can be found in writing, which one would like to put in one's own writing. So it may be that my writing has become a little denser, a little more multi-leveled than it once was, or perhaps this is merely due to the effect of experience and maturity, which allows me to focus on those things which I might not have done without teaching.

DS: So a writer who has time to work is going to produce a work of vastly greater depth than the bulk of writers, than any freelancer?

JEG: Well, let's take one example. For John Brunner the writing of *Stand on Zanzibar* (Hugo Award winner 1968—the ultimate overpopulation novel) was a very serious economic risk. He was only able to do it because a publisher was willing to advance him a considerable sum of money, having confidence in his ability to do this kind of work for which they could get back their advance, because John had to spend many more months on this book than he would have had to spend on any of the other books he writes. This sort of decision would not have been difficult for me. I would have been willing to spend the time necessary to produce the book if I could have written it—wish I had—because I do not have the economic pressure to keep producing work, to produce that which is easily saleable.

DS: Now that we are getting writers to take a chance, are we generally better off than we were twenty years ago when the field was more commercial? Are we presently living in the golden age of science fiction?

JEG: It's a matter of psychological viewpoint. The golden age is usually when one starts reading science fiction, because those are the stories which turn you on to science fiction and they have that aura of newness and the miraculous. There are a lot of exciting things going on, but I'm not sure at the moment whether they are of enduring value, and it remains to be seen. Only the future can look back on the present and say this was a golden age.

DS: Well, what do you have—what do you think will survive now? Any type and particular writer? What will become real classics?

JEG: Well, I think some writers, some works will become classics. I think Ursual Le Guin's *The Left Hand of Darkness* is one, and perhaps Frank Herbert's *Dune* is another. And perhaps *Stand on Zanzibar*, perhaps Robert Silverberg's *Dying Inside*. And there are many others. And the thing that sets these books apart is that they are primarily experimental. They're primarily statements of mature writers who are now writing at the top of their form, who are trying to do something more ambitious than they tried to do before, and I think they are succeeding, because obviously they have been recognized as broadly as writing something of exceptional merit.

DS: When you write a book, such as, say, *The Listeners*, what are you trying to do?

JEG: I was trying to write as good a novel as I could. But mainly I was trying to attempt something different. The general subject appealed to me. The image I suppose of people listening to voices from the stars, because it is a striking image. It gets back really to quite a basic dichotomy with man's hopes for the universe. The one hope, for instance, that we are the chosen, the elect, the only sentient creatures, the only ones favored by God and the universe, and we are alone. The other is the hope that we are not alone, that there are other people, other creatures intelligent enough to communicate with us, to share our dreams, to share our ideas and cultures with them. Just as in part of *The Listeners* I refer to the old problem of the human imagination, both in imagining a beginning to the universe and wondering what existed before that. Both of them are basic, contradictory images. They chase out the other one. Neither one of them is completely consistent, and out of this, I hoped to make *art*, a story people would want to read, about the basic problem, not only in the physical terms of listening for voices from the stars, but as well the basic problem between the individuals, between humans, communications at all levels. I tried to pair off the problems of interstellar communication with those of interhuman communication.

DS: Another place where you got in front of a large audience, aside from your books, was a television show based on *The Immortal*. Did you have a hand in that show and did you approve of what they did?

JEG: No. I had no hand in it. I sold the motion picture and TV rights to the book, and although I did have a little bit of influence with the scriptwriter who did the original motion picture of the week, which preceded the series by a year, I did not have any influence on the series itself. If you have read my *TV Guide* article on the subject you'll know that I thought it was pretty poorly done as a series. It sacrificed any SF value it might have, any appeal of the ideas, except for the basic concept of personal immortality which can be passed on to other people—sacrificed all those potentials in order to make another adventure show, another *Fugitive*.

DS: Do you think it was necessary to simplify sophisticated science fiction concepts for a mass audience? The producer certainly did.

JEG: No, I don't think it's true. I think that's a misconception on the part of the people who are in charge of making decisions like this, and I think that upon occasion, when the producers have not underestimated the intelligence or the appreciation of the audience they have come up with something which has been top rated and excellently done. For instance the Jacques Cousteau undersea specials, the works which have appeared on public broadcasting, the various series from England, the *Upstairs, Downstairs*, the *Civilisation* series, for that matter those which appeared on public television, the Alastair Cook's *America* series. Everytime something has been done with taste and intelligence I think it has been successful.

DS: Has anything been done with taste and intelligence in the science fiction field? Or is the first adult SF series yet to come?

JEG: Not consistently. I have seen a few shows that would—that I would have sat down and read as books. Certainly *Star Trek* had its moments, but they were not consistent and they were tied to a formula. There were occasional good shows on the science fiction and fantasy anthology shows back in the time when they were doing such things. But on the whole there has been nothing at which one can point and say, "This is outstanding science fiction."

DS: Have you had any other brushes with the visual media aside from *The Immortal*?

JEG: I had a story called "The Cave of Night" that was made into an hour television show on the old *Desilu Playhouse* back in 1959. It was a good production with E. G. Marshall and Lee Marvin but unfortunately they missed the whole point of the story.

DS: Have you ever done screenwriting yourself?

JEG: I have done some screenwriting, and one of my screenplays, or my one screenplay which was an adaptation of my story "The Reluctant Witch" came within a hair of being made into a movie. Actually they had started shooting when suddenly the money they were counting on didn't show up.

DS: So it was never produced at all?

JEG: No.

DS. Thank you, Mr. Gunn.

DS: You have something of a theatre background, don't you? How has this affected your fantasy writing?

FL: Well it's affected my writing in many ways, and from very early on. You see my father was a Shakespearean actor primarily on the stage, and so when I was just a little kid I was exposed to the plays of Shakespeare. I mean, my father was learning Hamlet when I was four years old. I learned the part pretty well at the time myself. But the main thing is that I was exposed to Shakespeare and to drama. I know that's had a profound effect on my writing. In the first place, I do at times tend to fall into a kind of Shakespearean poetry in my writing. And also I tend to cast stories in a dramatic form. I visualize scenes in my stories as if they were scenes in a play on the stage with entrances and exits, and I tend, as I said, to set my stories as if they were on the stage. Not too many of my stories have been dramatized but I've had a couple on Rod Serling's *Night Gallery*, and of course there's been *Conjure Wife*. I have not written for the stage, or television, or the movies, but I sometimes cast short stories in the form of one-act plays, with the stories consisting of stage directions and spoken dialogue. That's true of, say, "The Secret Songs" and "The Winter Flies" and "237 Talking Statues Etc."

DS: Do you think there's any potential in fantasy theatre?

FL: Yes, I think it's a possibility, and I'd like to see some of it done to my stories. A. J. Budrys pointed out that *The Big Time* just cries out for dramatization because it's done very much as a play, because it holds to the classical unities. It all happens in one place; it takes about two hours of actual story time; and there's a unity of motivation running through it. And as it happens right here at Brown University and out in Berkeley, California there are projects on at the present to dramatize *The Big Time* as a stage play.

DS: It seems to me that fantasy has a unique advantage on the stage, because the audience can be induced to imagine so much. Something done on stage, in the round, for example, with virtually no props, would be very difficult to do on screen because there you need elaborate special effects. *Peer Gynt* is a good example.

FL: Yes, whether things are done in that simple fashion, or whether there are attempts to use special effects on stage, I think it can be very impressive in both cases. If you do have special effects on stage, why, they have a kind of excitement that the movies and TV never had, because you're pulling out something right in front of the audience, like watching a magician work live. And so I think whether it's done by just letting the audience imagine the special effects, as is the case in theatre in the round, or whether you actually attempt it on stage, the results are always good.

DS: Do you think there would be an advantage here, because today the theatre audience is more discriminating than the movie audience, and you could actually get intelligent material produced?

FL: Yes, that's true. After all, even the movie audience is becoming more discriminating. The trend is towards small theatres and small audiences, and there isn't so much need for seeking the lowest common denominator audience nowadays on the stage or even in the movies. That's really the function of television.

DS: Have you had any experience writing for the movies?

FL: No, not really. And I've stayed away from it not because I don't want to do it but because I know it's a difficult sort of writing. Of course there are the technical problems and learning those in the medium, but also there is the problem of pleasing the people who are involved, the prospective producers, the ones who will pay for it, and the actors, and in the case of television the network and the sponsor. I've stuck to magazine and book fiction because that is still a one man job.

DS: Why do you write? Is it as a job, or for self expression?

FL: It's for both. Self expression is perhaps too weak a phrase. I write in order to stay sane. It's part of my whole adjustment to life, to be a writer, and look at experience from the point of view of hunting story material. If I couldn't write, I couldn't stay healthy, mentally and emotionally healthy. So, it's something I have to do and I have to do it for a living. I'm just at the age to be entering social security, but instead of having the retirement problem which can be so dreadful for some people, why I have no problem at all. I just gotta go on working, for support and for sanity.

DS: Then you find your writing more of a personal thing, not to be tampered with by others?

FL: I've gotten a great deal of help, really, from editors. I think John W. Campbell, Jr. certainly helped me a great deal with my first stories, and especially my first two novels, *Conjure Wife* and *Gather Darkness!* I submitted outlines and first chapters to him for those books, and he gave me a great deal of help. In the case of *Gather Darkness!* it was taking the characters more seriously and treating them as if they were real people rather than satirical figures, which they tended to be when I first started to write the book. And in *Conjure Wife* he helped me keep the plot from getting out of hand. Later on, almost ten years later, I found myself owing a great deal to Anthony Boucher. When I was selling to *Fantasy & Science Fiction* while he was editor he helped me give my stories more literary polish, more of a modern, contemporary treatment. There are several stories like "Rum Titty Titty Tum Ta Te" and "A Deskful of Girls," and "The Big Holiday" which wouldn't have their present form if it hadn't been for the intelligent cooperation of Tony Boucher. When he got my first versions of those stories he made suggestions of a most general sort for rewriting the stories. I'm happy to cooperate with the intelligent editor at any time. My stories have been improved by it. Some of my best titles, for instance, have been given me by editors. I owe a lot to Frederik Pohl there. For instance I had titled my story about chess as "Grand Master." I was thinking in terms of titles that would have appealed to John Campbell. He liked one word titles. And Fred Pohl picked out of the story the phrase, "The Sixty-Four Square Madhouse," and it made a fine title. That was true of "The Creature From The Cleveland Depths," which I had originally called "The Tickler," and Fred Pohl found this title in my story, and of course it's quite charming.

DS: What were your dealings with August Derleth like?

FL: They were always happy dealings, not always successful. Derleth rejected a number of my stories, oddly enough, that later sold successfully. I remember he turned down "The Man Who Made Friends With Electricity." Although it's quite a popular story and it was later selected by Judith Merril for best of the year and so on, Derleth didn't care for it. He didn't like fantasies with contemporary or topical materials in them, and political and social references. So we at times had difficulties there. He also rejected my Edgar Allan Poe story that was afterwards immediately bought by *Fantastic*. But although we had difficulties, I always enjoyed working with him, and I certainly wouldn't have gotten my Lovecraft articles into polished form, my articles like "Through Hyperspace With Brown Jenkin" and "A Literary Copernicus," except for the opportunity that Derleth's books provided. So we got along very well together. To tell the truth, when Derleth began his posthumous collaborations with Lovecraft, I was rather contemptuous of this idea of his. I thought that we oughtn't try to imitate and carry on Lovecraft in that particular fashion. But over the years I began to see that this enthusiasm was there, and my heavens, now we have a whole flood of Cthulhu Mythos stories, so that Bob Bloch denominated it as a whole sort of modern school which had grown from Lovecraft; and I also realize that without that sort of dogged enthusiasm Derleth would never have persisted in his efforts to make the critics and the general public aware of Lovecraft, which have in the long run proved so successful.

DS: Do you think this constant reuse of the Cthulhu Mythos is beneficial, or is there a danger of stagnation?

FL: [Laughs] That's a funny question. You know, for many years after Lovecraft's death I never would write a Cthulhu Mythos story. I had a feeling that this is just a sort of dead end, blind alley of writing, and I wanted to have no part in it. I finally went so far as to write "The Black Gondolier" in which I used, I think, Lovecraft's method of story construction, but of course I made no reference to the Cthulhu Mythos or any of the names and place names and entity names in Lovecraft's writing. And then about a year or so ago I wrote a pretty harsh review of Brian Lumley's *The Burrowers Beneath*, certainly a Cthulhu Mythos story *par excellence*. I took it apart and criticised it, and admitted my critical feeling about such stories. You know what the result of this was? I began to think, well, I'm a pretty weak character if I criticise something I haven't done myself. So I got tempted, and when Paul Berglund approached me, asking me to write a story for a book he was getting together for Donald Wollheim called *The Disciples of Cthulhu*, I finally decided I would try and write a Cthulhu Mythos story. And heaven help me, I've done it. So that pretty well answers your question.

DS: What has struck me as a problem is that the assorted Lovecraftian entities are no longer frightening when they become overly familiar. You know, a shelf full of *Necronomicons* is no more effective than one, and probably less so.

FL: Well, I've got an angle on that. My story is set back in 1936 and 1937, 1937 being the year that Lovecraft died. And by making it a period piece to that degree, I think I'm in a position at least to make the period come alive a little more. I'm putting it back in Lovecraft's time and it's a story that you might say Lovecraft might have written if he'd lived a few months longer.

DS: Did you have any contact with him while he was alive?

FL: Yes, I corresponded with him for the last eight months of his life, it turned out. That began exactly in the same way as Robert Bloch's contact with him. Robert Bloch first got in touch with Lovecraft by writing to inquire where he could obtain copies of Lovecraft's earlier stories. In my case my wife did it for me without my knowledge. She knew I was crazy about Lovecraft so she wrote to him, care of *Weird Tales* or *Astounding Stories*, and asked him where one could get hold of his earlier stories. And so he started to write letters to us and offered to lend them to us. There wasn't any need for that, it turned out. Then he asked me when I had sort of hinted that I'd written some stories in the weird vein, although I'd never sold anything, to let him see them immediately. Then he not only read them but critized them in a very friendly and considerate way, and also circulated my manuscripts among people like Henry Kuttner, Robert Bloch, August Derleth. In fact I wouldn't have met Bloch and Kuttner and Derleth if it hadn't been for Lovecraft circulating my stories, and so as I say this correspondence was voluminous. It had a big effect on my writing and continues to do so. So that was my main contact with Lovecraft.

DS: Are any of your early stories rewritten at Lovecraft's suggestion the way Bloch's "Satan's Servants" was?

FL: No, the only prose of mine that Lovecraft saw was "Adept's Gambit," the first Fafhrd and Mouser story I wrote, and Lovecraft made no suggestions for rewriting there. He merely corrected my spelling and made suggestions for better word choice in a few places. For instance I had talked about a door that was activated by hidden hinges, or by a hidden mechanism. He objected to the word "activate" and said "worked" or "moved" would be simpler and better. There you have Lovecraft coming out for the small word against the big word. In another case he objected to the use of "intriguing" to mean "fascinating." He said this was again almost a modernism. He sort of frowned on modernisms of this sort. But outside of that, no, he didn't make any suggestions for rewriting "Adept's Gambit." What did happen was this: I got so enthusiastic for a few months about Lovecraft that I did change "Adept's Gambit" slightly in one version and introduced references to Nyarlathotep and have something chanting "Ia Shug-Niggurath." Later on I realized that this was rather silly to try and stick the Cthulhu Mythos into the Fafhrd/Mouser stories, so I suppressed that version, which never was anything more than a manuscript. I had about four different versions of "Adept's Gambit" before it was finally published by Arkham House in my book *Night's Black Agents*.

DS: Was the Mouser series the first thing you ever wrote? How did you get started doing it?

FL: It grew up in my correspondence with Harry Otto Fischer. I was at the University of Chicago at the time, and I met another chap from Louisville, which was where Harry lived, named Franklin McKnight and McKnight introduced me to Harry. Harry and I hit it off and Harry began to write me long letters. I had never written at great length in my letters or anywhere else before then, but to keep up with the challenge presented by getting letters twenty and thirty pages long, why I began to write longer letters, and in our letters Harry and I began to create imaginary worlds, solely for the purpose of writing about them in our letters. We had really no idea at that time of making stories of them. So we invented several imaginary worlds together, and one of the imaginary worlds originally invented by Harry was the world of Fafhrd and The Grey Mouser, and the city of Lankhmar. Those things, Lankhmar, Fafhrd and

Mouser were invented in a couple of hand-written pages of Harry Fischer's letter. As we did with that sort of thing, I latched onto it and wrote him a reply, in which I told a little more about Fafhrd and the Grey Mouser, and we kept that up for a couple of years in our letters. But we never took it any further. We both began long stories, novels even, about these characters, and then abandoned them after a few dozen pages apiece. Then several years later Harry was working in the corrugated box business. He was a designer and engineer, and he had given up completely his earlier writing ambitions. But the magazine *Unknown* came along and with Harry's consent I tried a story for them about Fafhrd and the Mouser deliberately sort of fitting it into the pulp story vein, and fortunately that was successful and I carried on from there. But as it happened Harry has not collaborated with me except in one instance. I mentioned that Harry began a long novel which was called *The Lords of Quarmall*, and he wrote that one about 1935 and completed about 10,000 words of it. Then it became apparent to him that this was going to be two books long at least if he ever finished it, so he never did anything more with it. And twenty-five years later I finally decided that I was up to the job of taking these ten thousand words and writing a story around them that would also contain Harry's actual writing. And so I did that with my thirty-five thousand word version of it by the same title. Harry and I, at my suggestion, have simply split the income of that story on the basis of the wordage we contributed. He gets two sevenths and I get five sevenths of the profits, and that actually is just about the only collaboration that I've done.

DS: How do you feel about the sword and sorcery field in general? Do you think there's a danger of stagnation there too? You may remember that a couple of years ago Alexei Panshin called it a "literary fossil." How could it evolve?

FL: I don't know—I don't think it's a literary fossil any more than the detective story is a literary fossil. It's true it's generally set in what you might call a particular sort of past culture, but it seems to me that it's just subject to the dangers of all such fields. If there's too much slavish imitation of past stories, well then people probably will begin to find it sort of dull and the field won't prosper. But right now it seems to be going strong. I think as long as the writers remain inventive and don't try to write sword and sorcery stories according to some elaborate set of rules that have to be used in every story they'll do all right. I'm not in favor of limitations of that sort myself. All these genres of stories are just convenient pigeonholes for cataloging stories for libraries, and for the purposes of discussing them, of talking about them, but every story is a new creation, whether it's mainstream or some so-called genre, and so I think that the field for all I know may get stronger instead of fading out.

DS: In writing a Mouser story, which is more important to you, the characters or the world of Nehwon?

FL: Incidentally, Nehwon was invented by me in 1957 when Marty Greenberg brought out *Two Sought Adventure*, the first hardcover collection of the Fafhrd and Mouser stories, mostly ones that were published in *Unknown*, and it was then that I decided that the whole series needed a name, and so I invented Nehwon. As far as importance goes, the characters are a little more vivid, because I have tried to put them in other backgrounds. In fact earlier in "Adept's Gambit" I had the Alexandrian-Hellenic age as my background, but they're both pretty vivid.

DS: What is your basic method for creating an imaginary world?

FL: I can't rightly say that I have a basic method, because here my friend Harry Fischer performed the first act of creation. I have not followed the method of inventing the world carefully in the science fictional sense, I mean in deciding how big the planet is, what kind of gravity it has, what sort of atmosphere, how long are the years, how long are the days, and then working down to the actual forms of life, and the history of the culture of the dominant race. To tell the truth I have invented the world of Nehwon as I have gone along with the stories, and I have just now hinted in my last couple of stories, that there's a southern hemisphere to the world of Nehwon, but I've left it open as to whether it's a planet or a hollow world of some sort. I find on the whole that I like this method. It leaves me free. I haven't mapped out the entire world of Nehwon, so there may well be completely undiscovered continents. I haven't pinned things down, I don't have a history of Lankhmar that I refer to when I write a story about Fafhrd and the Mouser. I know as much as you'll find in the stories, and beyond that there's a grey mist.

DS: You mentioned the possibility of Nehwon being another planet. It seems to me that most fantasy settings, including yours, are just alternate versions of the Earth's past, without the history. Do you think it permissible to set a fantasy on another planet, and then have horses and oak trees, and that sort of thing?

FL: No, not if you're starting out with the idea that this is a story about another planet. I don't see how it's possible to use horses except when you're using one of the basic science fiction gimmicks, such as an interstellar empire, and the idea is that the Earth was colonised in the past, or sent out colonies in the past, and if you have colonies made up of not only human beings but horses, or if horses originated on some other planet and came here, well then maybe. If you start out from the science fiction premise I don't really see having horses on other planets. You could have animals that serve the same function as horses, but it would be more stylistic to have them derive from, oh, a reptilian stock, or some other stock that had no exact analogue on Earth.

DS: What fantasy writers, do you think had the most influence on your own work?

FL: E. R. Eddison, *The Worm Ouroboros*, has had a great influence on me. I think Robert Howard has, and certainly James Branch Cabell and the world of Jurgen and *The Cream of the Jest* were influential here. You were talking about *Peer Gynt* a while back, and I think that Ibsen and especially his fantasy, *Peer Gynt*, have had quite an influence on me. Those are some of the books. Dunsany, of course.

DS: Do you prefer to write fantasy as straight escapist fiction, or to use it as satire that way Cabell did?

FL: Oh I use it at times as satire and I like to link it with our modern world. For instance there's that story "The Bazaar of The Bizarre," and in it Lankhmar is menaced by some super-salesmen called The Devourers who are such dedicated salesmen that they hate to sell anything that's worth anything. They figure that the test of a salesman is that he can sell things that are utterly worthless, and this is a pretty obvious satire of Madison Avenue and the cheaper and more commercial side of Hollywood. I've gotten sort of a kick out of having smog in Lankhmar and calling it smog. Well they probably had smog in Rome and Babylon.

DS: Do you think that this ever destroys the effect of the fantasy, by popping the bubble?

FL: Yes, it can. It can. You have to be very careful with it. I get the impression from Ursula LeGuin's fine essay, "From Elfland to Poughkeepsie," that she feels strongly that some writers like Zelazny and myself are apt to do this sort of thing and pop the bubble. I don't feel we do, but that's really up to the readers and the critics to decide. If I have a character in Lankhmar say "Wow," if I do it the right way, that doesn't spoil the fantasy. All I'm saying is, yes, in Lankhmar that's the equivalent of "Wow!" and just as I have them talking English in my story I have them using equivalent words to some of our modern slang, and I don't feel that pops the bubble. But I think here it's a difficult problem and all you can decide is, "Does it work?"

DS: Do you find that your heavily satirical stories, such as *A Spectre is Haunting Texas*, date after a while?

FL: Yes, certainly. You do run up against the danger of such things dating. They reflect my own changing attitudes. I mean the only president for whose election I ever really worked was Johnson. I was in that Stop Goldwater business. A couple years after he got into office, though, Johnson was close to the top of my hate list and I wrote *The Spectre is Haunting Texas* to exorcise these strong feelings I had about Johnson and the Texas oil men, and so on. Then by the time the story came out Johnson wasn't running for president next time. He'd bowed out.

DS: It seems to me that the thing is good enough as a story to live on, and it might, if only people don't try too hard to dig out the topical references in it.

FL: Yes, I think that's true. There are topical references in all sorts of stories that were written five hundred or a thousand years ago, and we generally ignore them. But when the topical reference is to the recent past, then we're especially aware of how jarring it is. But in a hundred years who is going to worry about Johnson and Goldwater and the Democrats and Republicans of our particular era? It would probably just seem an oddity, and not a topical reference at all.

DS: Do you think your stories will be around a hundred years from now?

FL: I don't know. That's what we're all working for, of course.

DS: Thank you Mr. Leiber.

HAL CLEMENT

DS: How do you go about beginning to create an imaginary, yet scientifically plausible world for a science fiction novel?

HC: My usual start is from some astronomical source. I read a news squib in *Sky and Telescope* magazine or pick up something in a book, which seems interesting. There's something peculiar about the star, and I start to wonder what sort of planets it would have, and the rest is slide-rule and calculator work for quite a long time to come. But the inspiration is generally astronomical.

DS: What kind of technical knowledge do you need to do this?

HC: Well what I have is my basic astronomical knowledge. That was my major in college. I have a degree in it which is now thirty plus years old, but the basics still remain the same. You have to know the laws of celestial mechanics, the sort of factors which control how long it takes a planet to go around its star, which depends on the star's mass and its distance from the planet. You have to know enough of the laws of radiation to know what temperatures a planet of the given type would have at any given distance from the star. It's astrophysics basically, the laws of physics which apply to celestial bodies.

DS: Do you ever do it by starting with a scene or visually striking planetscape, then rationalizing it?

HC: I don't usually think of that aspect of it, no. I've done some stories which started from pictures, but that was something else again. Fred Pohl used to buy pictures which he liked, and which he thought he could use as covers, and then ship them out to writers to do a story around the picture. I did that five times, I think. But generally the spectacular side of it is there, and I'm not unaware of it, but you can make anything that's peculiar spectacular, so it's not really a very hard search.

DS: Would you tell us how you constructed the planet used in *Mission of Gravity* and *Star Light*?

HC: The thing that drove me there was perhaps not so much the astronomical facts but my contrary nature. Every time I hear someone use the words "of course" I start wondering what would happen if that particular "of course" weren't true. During my early science fiction fandom days I read stories of planets with lots of gravity or little gravity or ordinary gravity, but there was a sort of hidden "of course" there that said in effect that you could never have very different gravitational fields on the same planet. So I decided well it would be nice if you *could* have different gravities and I tried to find a way you can do it. From then on the slide rule came out again. The body involved happened to be available, the third whatever-it-is in the 61-Cygni system had been discovered, its orbit worked out pretty well. It was too faint and too low in mass to be seen as a star, and no one really knew for sure at that time whether something of that mass would be a star or a planet. At the moment the likelihood seems to be that it would be closer to star than planet. Instead of having the radiation equilibrium temperatures I gave it, it would probably have its own heat. What its temperature would be I don't know, but now that we know that Jupiter is putting out several times more heat than it gets, and this thing has several times the mass of Jupiter, I suspect if I did it again I would give it some very different qualities.

DS: I read about something like that recently, a body large enough to give off its own heat and support life. It just wandered around in interstellar space. Could something like that exist without a primary?

HC: Yes. There seems no reason at all to doubt it. I've written one such story myself. The present idea of how stars and planets formed is a snowballing theory, accretion theory. Material comes together, and if it has a mass on the order of the sun, it will develop central pressures and temperatures high enough to light a hydrogen fusion fire, and you have a star. If it's less than, I think present theories suggest five or six percent of the mass of the sun, then you do not get enough central temperature and pressure for hydrogen fusion. If it's much more massive than the sun you get a much brighter and hotter star. But there's no obvious reason why something couldn't accrete a very much smaller mass than a star. The Earth is like that. Whether it would be Earth-like in structure—I may have taken some chances there. I assumed in the story I wrote that the body had formed out in the Orion area which is rich in gas and dust and young stars. I assumed that it was at least a second and possibly a third generation object. That is, the material which made it had already been cycled through stars once or twice. It would therefore be rich in heavy elements. And I assumed that the thing had developed heat enough when it did come together, either from potential energy or from radioactive energy, to cook off most of the hydrogen, as took place here on the Earth, and I therefore wound up with a planet not grossly different from the Earth. Like enough so that a human being could stand the gravity; I think it was about one and a half G's. He couldn't breathe the air, which was heavily ammonia and hydrozene vapor, and the natural life was richer in nitrogen than our own. It was basically carbon life, but the liquids it used for solvents were ammonia and hydrozene.

DS: If such a planet were in interstellar space, it would receive no solar radiation. Wouldn't that make a big difference?

HC: In that particular case it had star light. There were a few of the O-type stars of the Orion region within half a lightyear or so. It was too dark for my human character. The most noticeable thing in the sky aside from some very bright stars was the Orion nebula, which covered a good deal of the sky, and the fellow carried a flashlight but he had problems in using it because the lifeforms on the planet could not stand photons as energetic as he needed to see by. They saw by long wavelength stuff, infra-red light, and would get a probably fatal sunburn from a few seconds exposure to an ordinary flashlight. So my character's native friend had to guide him, and he had to accept the guidance because he couldn't use his flashlight except under the most restricted conditions.

DS: What story was this?

HC: It was called the "The Logic of Life." It appeared in Ballantine's *Stellar*.

DS: When you have already created a planet, what then do you do for a story?

HC: The story is, I'm afraid, pretty much of an afterthought with me. When I have the planet pretty well worked out I think of as many non-standard things as I can think up that would happen on it, in what ways it would be different from Earth. Generally I write these things down on index cards, and when the pile of cards is high enough I begin laying them out on the floor or on a card table or something, and I try to put them into some sort of chronological sensible order, and eventually I have a story.

DS: This seems rather cut and dry. What do you do for characters?

HC: They're sort of incidental. I suspect a lot of critics will tell you that my characters aren't much to write home about. To me that's more mechanical than anything else. Something is going to happen, and if I can figure out any basic motivation for people being there at all, then the other basic motivations such as survival and curiosity will generally provide the doings of a story. I can't answer that one very well, and some people say the motivations I stick in my characters are not very sensible. In *Mission of Gravity* there is a nice economic one. They had sent x-billions of dollars of apparatus down to the high gravity region of Mesklin and the stuff had failed to lift off again, so they had a pretty good motive for at least getting their investment back. The motivation of the native was something else again, and it was part of the story. Based on my personal sort of idealism, that knowledge is important to intelligent forms. I made Barlennan's sneaky activities based on his wish to get hold of alien science.

DS: Do you ever try and concentrate on building up characters as personalities, asking *to whom* something is going to happen?

HC: I try to, but I don't consider that I'm very good at it. My human characters particularly don't mean very much to me. Someone like Barlennan in *Mission of Gravity*, who showed up again in *Star Light*, I have a fairly good idea of his character. I hope it's a consistent one. People who read both books can decide for themselves. He's a sort of sharp trader type, a quick deal artist. He knows what he wants and he's going out in quite a lot of directions to get it. He's not always very ethical about it by—I would have said human standards, but the human standards in that direction have been going downhill for quite a while now, so maybe that's a poor comparison.

DS: Have you ever felt the inclination to write pure fantasy, in which you could construct new physical laws for a universe?

HC: The temptation has been there. The trouble is that my own tendency is to be so strongly consistent internally that I've never buckled down to the work. The moment I change one of the things I regard as a natural law, a lot of corollaries change also, and I tend to get lost in figuring out what else would have to be true before this change operated. So I've generally gotten bogged down before I did very much developing and I've never written such a story. Maybe I'll get to it sometime.

DS: Early in your career, did you ever want to write for *Unknown*?

HC: Not very strongly. *Unknown* got going just about the time I did. I was not a fantasy enthusiast at the time and I didn't begin reading *Unknown* until practically the end of its career.

DS: How did you get started?

HC: I got started in writing rather gradually. A friend of mine introduced me to science fiction magazines when I was about ten. I started buying them when I was about twelve, and began telling the stories at boyscout campfires, and gradually feeling that I would have had things happen differently if I had written it. When I was seventeen or eighteen I began trying to write. Just bits and drabs. I didn't finish a real story. When I was nineteen I did finish one. John Campbell bought it.

DS: How did John Campbell work with you to get you to bring out your abilities?

HC: In general there wasn't too much detailed work. I saw him two or three times. We would have conversations, which as was usual with John, were sometimes of a rather argumentative nature. He would point out some things which might or might not be true, and let me go on my own. I think the story which was most completely due to John Campbell was "Technical Error." He had suggested a number of strictly engineering things which might be done differently from what we do here on the Earth, and I used the old abandoned spaceship ploy in which the engineering had been done in those oddball ways, and faced my human characters with the problem of finding out how to work the thing.

DS: You mean the idea was mostly his?

HC: In that particular story the specific things about bringing surfaces together, having the surfaces so thoroughly smooth that they would cling by intermolecular forces when you brought them together, of using magneto-striction to change the shape of things so they would fit under one set of circumstances and not under another. Those were specifically John's ideas.

DS: I know he often would feed out ideas to writers and tell them to write stories around them, such as when he gave Asimov the idea of "Nightfall." Did he ever approach you with anything like that?

HC: No more specifically than "Technical Error." Others, it's very hard to tell how much was John Campbell because over the years I saw a fair amount of him. He'd come up to Boston every year or so, telephone a bunch of us, and we'd go over to a hotel room and shoot the breeze for a good many hours. We frequently disagreed on things, but it's really impossible for me to say now how much of a given story came out of points that were flung around at some of those discussions.

DS: What was your general impression of him as an editor?

HC: He was an extremely competent man. He knew what he wanted to do and was able to do it. The success of *Astounding* and later *Analog* under his leadership seems sufficient evidence for that. I didn't always agree with him, heaven knows, very few people did. But he had his ideas and was able to carry them out. He was a good, competent man.

DS: Right now are you still writing actively?

HC: I'm as active as I ever have been. Writing for me is a hobby. A high school science teacher is my vocation. That's where I support my family and generally get my bread, you might say, without the butter. Science fiction writing and science fiction and astronomical painting provide the butter on the bread perhaps, justifying my going to science fiction conventions and things of that sort.

DS: You've done astronomical painting?

HC: Yes. I don't use my own name for the painting. I fell in love with astronomical art of the Chesley Bonestell variety years ago, but when you see the stuff at conventions, then look at the minimum bid they put on it, you drool and walk away. I eventually got tired of drooling and went out and bought myself some paints and while I never had any artistic training outside of high school, I found that I could do planetary scenes and astronomical scenes well enough so that people would buy them. I've sold between seventy-five and eighty paintings in the last four years or so.

DS: What name do you do them under?

HC: The name I use is George Richard. I don't really care who knows anymore. I started with another name because I wanted to find out if the pictures were good enough for people to buy them for their own sake, or were just going to buy them because they were by a name author.

DS: Did you ever think of doing cover art for books?

HC: Not seriously. It would mean painting to a deadline, and as with the writing, the painting is strictly spare-time stuff. I don't have all that much time for it, especially during a school year.

DS: Does this ever affect your fiction? Have you ever painted a scene, then later written a story about it?

HC: I haven't done it yet, but it seem quite likely that it will happen. I have painted some scenes for the same basis that I did stories, that is, as I mentioned earlier, something that I have seen in *Sky and Telescope* magazine. I'm going to paint one at the moment from an article in *Scientific American* on x-ray binary stars. Whether I'll do a story about it afterwards, I don't know. I've just been doing a good deal of calculating in order to make the painting reasonable. I haven't put brush on canvas yet. It's a picture I'm planning.

DS: Have you ever thought of trying to arrange to do the illustrations and cover for your own work?

HC: Not seriously. It is a time question again, and if I tried to do anything of that sort it would just commit me to time I can't very well spare. I did a chapter on Jupiter for a book of Ben Bova's which he now has and I included a painting of my own of what I thought the red spot area would look like close up, and sent it on to him, but I seriously doubt he'll use it. I'm not even sure he knows it's by me. I used the George Richard name on the back of the painting.

DS: It would seem that if you can paint well enough to sell paintings, this could give you complete control of the package on one of your books, rather than leaving it to some other cover artist who may or may not know what he's doing.

HC: This is true but I'm not all that sure it means that much to me. I don't worry that much about it. Some cover paintings that I've seen have bothered me. Some have been perfectly okay. There has been one artist and only one, so far, who consulted me before he finished the painting. That was Rich Sternbach who did the *If* cover for "Mistaken For Granted" a couple of years ago. Otherwise I've never had any say and no one has ever asked me, and in general the results have been all right. In some cases I have wanted to get hold of the paintings. In one case I paid a fairly stiff sum to get hold of the Kelly Freas cover paintings for *Star Light*.

DS: Did you ever have a case where the cover painting was bad in a certain edition and the book didn't sell?

HC: There have been quite a variety of cover paintings, and I generally don't know if it bombed or not. There was an edition of *Needle* that had a very strange cover, quite hard to describe really, and it didn't send me particularly, but I have no idea whether that particular printing went well or not. *Cycle of Fire* was just reissued by Ballantine and Judy-Lynn did send me a proof of the painting after it had been bought and the plates made and everything, and asked if I liked it—which I did. It was a very nice painting. I hope I can get my fingers on that original sometime. I can't think of any which I really regarded as bad.

DS: How do you feel about interior illustrations? Does this aid the reader in building up a mental picture of the story, or does it hinder it?

HC: I'm sure it aids it. The amount of aid would vary enormously from one person to another. Some people may get their visualizations from my words before they turn to the page that has the picture on it, and they might get quite jolted. But that's a matter of not who's right, but who communicated better.

DS: On occasion you have done stories which had nothing to do with astronomy. What, for example, moved you to write *Ocean on Top*?

HC: That was one of the stories that Fred Pohl bought as a cover and asked me to do. He had purchased a painting, a fairly traditional undersea thing with a big domed city in the background, and a couple of scuba-armored figures swimming around in the foreground with bubbles coming out of them. He sent me a photostat of the painting, black and white; he put red pencil around the two swimming figures, cutting out the city, and said he wanted to print this much of the picture upside down with the bubbles going down, and can you write me a story Hal?

DS: And you wrote an entire novel around that cover?

HC: Well, this was a little of a surprise. I had a two week spring vacation coming up, and I said, sure I'll try it at maybe ten thousand words, but the thing kept growing on me. It overran spring vacation by a week or two, and wound up at a little over fifty thousand, which was novel length. I think Fred was a little surprised. I'm not sure even to this day whether he bought it because he liked it or because he thought he was stuck with it. It was several years before anybody bought the book rights to it. I admit I was experimenting in several ways at once in that story, and I'm willing to admit that the experiments were not wholly successful. It's far from being my favorite among my own work.

DS: Do you ever find yourself having written a story, maybe many years ago, that now you would rather bury?

HC: There are some that I don't think much of. As I look back—my memory is not nearly what it used to be—there are none which I would—no I'll take that back. There is one juvenile novel I did under contract to a publisher who promptly failed after he put it out, and if no one ever mentions that one again I'd be just as happy. Since very few people know about it, it's all right.

DS: Was it under your own name, or a pseudonym?

HC: It was under the Clement pseudonym.

DS: Why have you so consistently used the Clement pseudonym?

HC: I kept using it because it had commercial value eventually. I used it originally because when I sold my first story to John Campbell I was an undergraduate at Harvard, I had done a couple of articles for *Sky and Telescope* magazine, which at that time was published at Harvard Observatory, and I was a little leery about the possible reactions of the director of the place, Harlow Shapley, and my faculty advisor Donald Menzel, to the possibility of having the same name appear in their dignified astronomical publication and in a pulp magazine. By the time I found out that they both tried to write science fiction themselves and wouldn't have minded in the least, Hal Clement was a name to stay with.

DS: Did you ever have any problem with science fiction not being respectable? You know, hiding it in a plain brown wrapper and all that?

HC: It was never a problem. I don't think my parents thought much of it, but they certainly didn't react to is as they would have if it had been a copy of *Spicy Detective*, which in those days was regarded as pretty bad. No, they let me go my own way in that respect. I think my father wanted me to be a minister, but he settled on my going into science, and admitted many years later that I'd done the right thing. So, no I never had to hide the magazine. As clearly as I can remember I was in grammar school when I began buying them regularly, and I would go up during lunch hour to the drugstore a few blocks away and if the new *Wonder Stories* had come in I would buy it and bring it back to school. My teachers may not have approved, but none of them ever tried to take it away from me or suggest that I ought to buy something of higher quality for my two bits.

DS: Well that's unusual. That happened to *me* when I was in high school, and that was 1970.

HC: Not all teachers are that narrow, I like to believe, being a high school teacher myself.

DS: Then how do you feel about the current academic interest in science fiction?

HC: It's good in a way. It's nice to be respectable, I suppose. I'm not quite so happy with some of the people who have popped into it and set themselves up as science fiction experts. Ben Bova's editorial on that subject a few months ago, I think, covers the point much better than I can. There are people teaching science fiction courses who are not really aware that anyone ever lived except Poe and Verne.

DS: Do you think this is because they don't think science fiction requires such rigorous scholarship?

HC: This is because we are so early in the field in a time of respectability that no one is quite sure what constitutes professional competence, and there are a lot of departments who feel that your established professional competence in general literature means more than years of experience as a science fiction fan. Not all of them feel that way but quite a few of them apparently do.

DS: Have you been approached to teach a science fiction course or speak at one?

HC: Yes. Both. I was asked in the high school where I teach last year if I would take on a science fiction course for a term, and I said I was for it in principle if they could find the time in my schedule, which they could not. Then for about three years I taught an evening course in science fiction at a very small college in my home town. The take wasn't very great; there were never very many people in the course, and they didn't offer it again this year, and I was just as happy because it can kill one evening a week very very dead with all the preparation that had to be done. I've spoken quite often to school groups on science fiction. Only last week I drove from Boston to a town in Pennsylvania where I spent the entire day at a school, where they are teaching science fiction courses. I addressed four different classes in science fiction courses, one in a literature and other arts course, and cleaned up the day by talking to the local science fiction club.

DS: What is your impression of these classes? Do they ask you intelligent questions, or do they ask the usual run of cliches?

HC: My experience has been that they tend to be pretty imaginative. The cliches are there of course. You can never get rid of them, and some of the questions are standard, but even though they are standard, I still wouldn't call them cliches. A high school kid asking what gives you ideas or how do you build up a story is a perfectly legitimate and sensible question, and the fact that I have had to answer it many times before doesn't reflect on the questioner. He hasn't heard my answer.

DS: Are you generally pleased with the direction science fiction is taking now?

HC: Generally. Yes. There are some aspects of it I have never been able to get enthusiastic about, the so-called "new wave" never sent me very much. I'm essentially old-fashioned. I still like space opera. In a sense that's what I write.

DS: No two people ever really agreed on what the "new wave" is or was. What's your working definition?

HC: I never really worked out a verbal definition of it either. It was science fiction stories in which people got very, very involved with personality crises, or identity crises. They were more psychological than physical in their science. And, without wanting to belittle the importance of the psychological sciences, I'm not sure they're well enough developed to justify writing stories about them in which you can say it really would have happened this way.

DS: Can you ever say that about anything?

HC: You can come a lot closer. You can at least calculate reliably what the gravity of a planet with a given mass and radius is going to be. You can calculate reliably what its temperature is going to be if you know how far it is from what kind of star. I agree that beyond that you've got to have human behavior among your characters, but some of the types of behavior that turned up in the so-called "new wave" were built so far out on scaffoldings of psychological speculation that they lost their believability in many cases.

DS: Do you still recognize these as science fiction then?

HC: Yes, you get to the point where I would hesitate to call them science fiction. There are some very good stories, not "new wave" by any sense of the word, which are to my feeling not science fiction either. Most of what Ray Bradbury has written, his *The Martian Chronicles* for example, was as unscientific as one could get. Ray knows this perfectly well and doesn't care. I admire him beyond words as a master of the story-teller's craft, but I don't think what he writes is science fiction in my admittedly rather narrow and old fashioned idea of what that means.

DS: Do you think it is detrimental to the field to stuff science fiction anthologies full of stories which are not science fiction? Will this lose readership?

HC: I can't tell what will lose readership. Any story which a certain editor felt was good, presumably a number of readers are going to feel is good. I don't see why having a wide variety of stories in an anthology is going to hurt it. I should think it would almost have to help it. You would hope that any reader will realize that if there are ten different stories in the book he is probably not going to like all of them, and why worry about it? It's a matter of subjective tastes there.

DS: What are your subjective tastes in science fiction? What writers do you admire?

HC: I like Larry Niven, at least when he's out in space. I like Poul Anderson very much. Those are two names which immediately jump to mind. But they're both the hard science fiction types, as close to the old style space opera as you can get.

DS: Do you find that the old style space opera holds up on rereading?

HC: Yes. I still reread Doc Smith, Jack Williamson's *Legion of Space*, and stories of that sort, and I still enjoy them.

DS: Wouldn't you agree though that the modern writers of the same sort write with considerably more skill and sophistication?

HC: That's probably a fair statement. Larry Niven knows more astronomy than Doc did. Smith had his Ph.D in chemistry, not astronomy. I'm not sure that beyond that he is a better writer. There are a lot of faults which can be held against E. E. Smith at this point. They talk about his cardboard characters, and that sort of thing. Well I don't know. He had mastered the art of knowing how to keep things happening in the story. He kept and can still keep a reader's attention, and this is the essential of the craft.

DS: Were you ever disturbed by his apparent inability to get his heroes into danger? For example, at the end of *Galactic Patrol* he resolves everything by putting Kinnerson in bulletproof armor and sending him in to shoot up the bad guys. This is not my idea of meaningful conflict.

HC: If you're implying there was no danger, I don't think you have analyzed the situation very well. His character had protected himself as well as he could against the foreseeable dangers, but he knew perfectly well that there were others he might not have been able to foresee, and if I had been in his position, and I have been in comparable positions, I'm sure I would have been just as scared. The Smith characters have been criticized. As far as I'm concerned they never bothered me very much. I may be a little bit of a mid-Victorian idealist myself. Feelings like love and courage and loyalty which are down-graded by a lot of people nowadays still mean a great deal to me.

DS: What about his inability to write dialogue the way people talk?

HC: The way people talk *when*? Styles of what is cliche and what is sensible talk have varied enough during my lifetime so that I am extremely aware of them. It seems to me that many of the conversations which have been belittled in *Galactic Patrol* or *Second Stage Lensman* are perfectly sensible, making allowance for the way the people would feel at that time. I know I wouldn't talk that way right now, certainly not to someone twenty or twenty-five years younger than I am, but I can conceive of situations in which I would talk that way. And quite possibly I do, and although I'm not aware of being laughed at behind my back, I am aware that my attitude on such things is quite a long way from being up to date.

DS: Did you ever feel inclined to design a future idiom for a story?

HC: Not to any great extent. I have sometimes invented a term or two which will apply to the situation, but if there is anything that is unpredictable, I'd say it would be slang.

DS: What areas of the sciences which you are familiar with seem to provide the most exciting possibilities for speculation?

HC: Astronomy and astrophysics still, especially the far-out part of it, cosmology, what quasars are and so on. Biochemistry and the details we're picking up on that. Those I would say are the two most prominent sources for the imagination.

DS: Have you ever written anything in the biological area?

HC: I did. It was called "The Mechanic." It appeared in *Analog* about 1966 and was in a collection of my stuff called *Small Changes* which came out

from Doubleday about 1969.
DS: Thank you.

L. SPRAGUE DE CAMP

DS: Why did you decide to become a writer?

LSDC: I lost my job. It's a very simple answer. What happened was that I had a friend in New york, who, during the Great Depression in order to continue to eat started writing stories for the science fiction magazines, of which he was a more faithful reader than I was. I was working at the International Correspondence School in Scranton at the time, and used to come in every month or so and pay my friend a visit. He had been my college roommate. His name is John D. Clark. He's now a retired chemist. I helped him with plotting a couple of these stories, and to everybody's surprise he sold them. Well, I thought, if he can do it, why can't I? So in my spare time I wrote a couple, and to my great surprise they sold too. Well, my reaction of course was *wheee!* Why hadn't somebody told me about this before? It sure beats working. I left my job in Scranton to take another one at a somewhat better salary—I think it was all of $1650 a year, which was a living wage in those days—in New York City. After three months I lost that job in an economy purge. The boss was very apologetic about it, but he was a real character out of . . . well, let's say he was a capitalist out of *The Daily Woikah* . . . if you know what that means. Later he landed in an insane asylum, where he was kept in a padded cell as a dangerous paranoiac. So then I thought that if I could spend five hours a week on my own writing stories and make so much money, why if I could spend fifty hours a week I'd make ten times as much. Now there's a fallacy in there because you seem to run into a law of diminishing returns, but nevertheless I took a crack at freelancing, and except for the Second World War and a few temporary jobs, I've been at it ever since.

DS: When did you first come into contact with John Campbell?

LSDC: John Clark got to know Campbell and introduced me to him. He invited a number of people around to his apartment one night for a little party, and that party included Campbell. Campbell had not yet become the editor of *Astounding*. He was still freelancing himself. This was about 1937.

DS: When he became editor, how much influence did he have over what you wrote?

LSDC: He had a great deal, and he also had a good deal of influence in teaching me how to get along with editors, and how to make up and submit manuscripts, and the mechanical details of that sort. He did not have so much influence over me as he did with some people, because I have never been very good at taking other people's ideas and writing stories about them. And of course he was full of ideas which he would pass around among his various authors, but I found that it usually worked better when I relied on my own originality for the ideas. I believe there was one story that I did write that he suggested the plot for. That was called "The Ghosts of Melvin Pye." He said, "How would it be if a man was a split personality, and when he died he had two ghosts?" So that was the story, but *he* rejected it, by the way. It finally appeared in another magazine.

DS: I note that when you started to write for him, you moved from short stories to novels. Did he specifically try to train you for longer work?

LSDC: No, not particularly. Actually I had started work at the time in collaboration with the late P. Schuyler Miller, who was a long time friend of mine, on a novel which eventually appeared as *Genus Homo*, which has been in and out of print ever since. And although it looks fairly crude as I look it over today, nevertheless we must have done something right. The plot is essentially the same as that of *Planet of The Apes*. In fact the resemblance was so close that I sometimes wondered if Pierre Boulle hadn't seen it at some stage in his career.

DS: In what way do you find it crude?

LSDC: Well, the phony names, for example, that I give the civilized gorillas. They were very amateurish effects. I'm sure I could do a lot better. You see, one of the troubles of freelance writing over a long period is that when you are young you have lots of original ideas. They come faster than you can write them down. But you don't know how to express them in just the right way, and the result is often pretty bad. But then when you get older, your work acquires more and more polish and you learn how to put sentences together in the best possible way and everything, but the ideas don't come quite so easily.

DS: How do you feel about most of your early work? It seems to me that something like *Lest Darkness Fall* holds up very well.

LSDC: There again, when I look it over today I have sort of an itch to grab for an editorial pencil and make a whole lot of little changes in it, but since the thing has been in print for so long, I must have done something right.

DS: Eventually you drifted away from writing for Campbell. Why was this?

LSDC: He put it to me one time when I was turning out stuff faster than he could buy it. He said, "Well you know, Sprague, you can write *for* the magazine, but you can't write the magazine." So I started sending stuff elsewhere, since I was turning it out quite fast at that time, and also some of the stories that I sent him he rejected, so I tried them on the other magazines. I very early learned the first principle of magazine writing, which is try for the best paying outlet first, and if it bounces from that one, why you go down the line.

DS: Do you sometimes feel that the best markets aren't always buying your best work? That something bounced way down the line that shouldn't have?

LSDC: Who is to say what's best? It's a subjective judgment, and a story that I particularly happen to like may not appeal to other people at all. It all depends. We all have our individual preferences and prejudices, and editors can't avoid having them, no matter how hard they try to be objective in the matter. Of course, if the manuscript is only semi-literate, why nearly everybody will agree that it is not suitable for publication. But assuming that it's reasonably literate and is turned in in proper form, and is not full of glaring grammatical errors or obvious fictional blunders—and if you want to know what's an obvious fictional blunder, Catherine and I have said a great deal about them in *The Science Fiction Handbook, Revised*—it's a matter of individual opinion. So there have been some of my stories that apparently I liked better than the best-paying editors. They usually got published eventually, but I don't think anything of mine that is really worth publishing has failed to find a berth sooner or later.

DS: Have you ever run into problems with editors who want stories along a specific line? I'm thinking specifically of the late-1950s *Astounding*, which seemed to be three-quarters psionics stories.

LSDC: This does present a problem, though not in my case a very serious one. But I have run into some curious little quirks and prejudices. John Campbell, for example, among other things, would not publish a story in which an extra-terrestrial species was portrayed as superior to human beings in a general sense. That is, morally, mentally, and physically better all around. He just didn't like that. And he was somewhat of an old-fashioned imperialist also. He thought that the United States ought to go and conquer all of Latin America. He had some rather curious ideas of that sort. When Horace Gold was editing *Galaxy*, the magazine got the name of "psychiatric science fiction" because of Horace's strong interest in that direction. But on the whole I wouldn't say I have been very much bothered. I do know that I once did a story which has been rewritten and expanded and published as *The Great Fetish*, and Campbell bounced that because I had some of the characters commit fornication in it. It wasn't done on stage; it was done very tactfully and all that sort of thing. There wasn't a dirty word in it. But there was a reference to creaking bedsprings and something like that, and he kept Katie Tarrant there as sort of his watchdog to catch anything that was the least bit sexy.

DS: Something very similar goes on in *Lest Darkness Fall*, and he bought that.

LSDC: I'm not sure that it was in the magazine version, because I expanded the novel considerably for book publication.

DS: What was your overall impression of Campbell as an editor?

LSDC: I thought he was an excellent one. He had his quirks and his short-comings, but when you discount those he was about the best all-around editor of imaginative publications that there has been so far. And I'm very grateful to him for helping me get started. He and Fletcher Pratt and my 1941 attendance at the Breadloaf Writers' Conference had about as much affect on training me as anything.

DS: What was the most valuable thing he ever taught you?

LSDC: One thing he taught me which is not really literary is: don't go around to an editor who doesn't like your stuff and say, "But it must be good because I've worked so hard on it." There's no necessary connection.

DS: What went on at the 1941 Breadloaf Conference?

LSDC: There were lectures on the various aspects of professional writing by Fletcher Pratt, the late Bernard de Voto, and a number of other people of that stature. I took pretty careful notes on them, and actually much of what I heard there forms the basis for *The Science Fiction Handbook*.

DS: Was there anything like a modern SF writers' workshop in which they pass around everybody's stories for extensive criticism?

LSDC: I've heard of such, but I've never been through that particular mill myself. I did go to the Milford Conference one year, but I didn't bring a manuscript along to be criticized, so my part in the proceedings was sort of marginal.

DS: Why did you shift away from science fiction at the end of the 1950s?

LSDC: Mainly because there were several other kinds of writing that I thought I could do which would provide more wealth and glory. Those included popularizations like *The Ancient Engineers* and historical novels like *An Elephant for Aristotle*. I also did quite a lot of article writing. I was a pretty regular

55

contributor to *Science Digest* for a number of years. And I did continue to write a certain amount of fantasy, mostly my work on the Conan series. So I was never out of the imaginative field altogether; I just sort of dropped science fiction in the strictest sense. I might have done more if Campbell hadn't indicated that he wasn't interested in any more of my Krishna novels, which are of a kind you might call "sword and planet." It all started pretty much with Edgar Rice Burroughs's Barsoomian tales, and in rereading some of those I thought, well now look, I could do that, but do it in a more modern and better informed way than Burroughs did. So I tried it out and tried to keep things logical, which Burroughs never bothered about, and that series was the result. But apparently Campbell's own interests shifted away from that sort of thing in *Astounding*, and nobody else either showed enough interest or wanted to take serials, or was paying well enough to make it worth my while. So I tried out these other things and had some degree of success in them. Not in the historical novel field unfortunately. I wrote five of them. Doubleday published them all in hardcover, and they've all been through paperback. Unfortunately, I got into that field just at the wrong time, when it had started down from its peak of popularity in the 1950s. As a result, although I must say the critics were very kind and indulgent on the whole to these novels, each one sold less well than the one before. So when the last one, *The Golden Wind*, appeared in 1969 and performed in that manner, I said "To hell with this. I won't write any more of these unless market conditons change." I have ideas for a couple of more, but I don't intend to put in the time on them unless the chances of profit are a good deal greater.

DS: Would you ever write something just because you wanted to, even though you might make more money at something else? Assuming, of course, that the work could be published, even though it might not be as profitable?

LSDC: Yes, yes, but what I write of that sort mainly consists of little articles and light verse for fan magazines. But when it comes to writing something of book length, which may take anywhere from three months to two years, well I have to think about what the commercial possibilities are. After all, authors have to eat just as other people do, you know.

DS: Have you ever reached the stage where because of a backlog of material which stays in print and generates royalties, you can do anything you want?

LSDC: Let's say that I'm not doing too badly now, since Conan started taking off, and I probably could afford to write a whole book that didn't promise great commercial rewards. As a matter of fact I've had such a book in mind for some time, and that's a book on civilization. The same title as Lord Clark's, only mine would be spelled with a 'z.' I've been collecting material on the subject of what you might call the causes and cures of civilization for the last quarter century and I have quite a mass of stuff now. But whether I shall get around to writing it, I don't know, because people keep asking me to write other things. Another trouble in the business is that when you are young, nobody wants your stuff and you have to scurry around and you're very grateful if you can make fifteen dollars for a piece in some obscure publication, but then when you get along and have acquired a backlog, why everybody wants you to do something for them at once. Unfortunately, I don't have the property attributed to some Catholic saints of being in two places at once. I had to turn down a nice enough offer to do an article on a fairly easy subject just yesterday, because between the remaining Conan novel I have contracted to do for Conan Properties, Inc. and the Robert Howard biography, and another article I have promised, I have enough to keep me busy for quite a few months. Probably the rest of the year.

DS: Could you tell us something about the Robert E. Howard biography?

LSDC: The present title is *Dark Valley Destiny: The Life & Death of Robert E. Howard*, and I'm writing it in collaboration with Dr. Jane Whittington Griffin, a child psychologist at the University of Pennsylvania. She specializes in developmental problems and things like that, and by a curious coincidence Catherine and I discovered that Dr. Griffin comes from Eastland, Texas, and knows people who knew the Howard family, and knows a lot of the people around there. That more or less got us started, because before that I thought, well, Robert's very interesting, but I just don't think there's enough information available on him because of the shortness of his life to support a full length book. But with Dr. Griffin's psychological analyses of him and all the leads she was able to give us, why we expect to have a book almost as big as the Lovecraft biography. In the summer of 1977, she and Catherine and I flew down to Texas and spent some weeks driving around in a van borrowed from Jane's brother, who is an M.D. in Fort Worth, with tape recorder and camera, running down leads and taping interviews. Unfortunately a week before we took off, I had very stupidly fallen down stairs and broken my coccyx and cracked one rib, so I drove this monster over the magnificent distances of Texas while sitting on an inflated rubber doughnut and let's say it was an interesting expedition, but not a very relaxing one. The temperature was 107 at the Dallas-Fort Worth Airport when we left.

DS: What sort of new information did you uncover?

LSDC: That depends on what you mean by new. New for whom? We got it from various people. We have had contacts with all of Robert's surviving relatives that we can run down, cousins and such, and also various people who lived in Cross Plains in his time and remember things about him. So, as you see, we have quite a sizable mass of information, besides of course all his own writings and a set of copies of his letters. We find that we have to exercise a little caution in using his letters, though, because Robert, like his father, didn't believe in spoiling a good story for the sake of a few facts.

DS: How much of what he told about in his letters—such as his alleged brawls—did you find to be factual, and how much was a good story?

LSDC: I'm afraid those are a good story, because I quizzed several of his friends on the subject, and they said that they were purely imaginary. He was known to get drunk occasionally. He did drink, mostly beer. He occasionally got drunk, but it was never anything like a wild brawl. If he got a little lit up he might take a book and sit down in a corner somewhere and read, because he was a tremendous reader, and a great deal of the time when he describes himself as dashing around the countryside and performing deeds of derring-do like raiding schoolhouses in order to borrow books from them in the summertime—well that apparently never happened. He was at home reading all the time. Furthermore, he didn't start his body-building exercises until 1927, when he was 21 years old. Also his hints at wenching are probably purely fictitious. In one of his letters to Lovecraft he talked about it. Robert had been selling stories to *Spicy Adventures*, you see, although by modern standards they're as mild as milktoast, and he wrote Lovecraft and said, "I based it on one of my own sexual adventures. Why don't you do the same sort of thing?" Well you can just imagine poor HPL cringing at such a suggestion. But as far as I can see, his sexual adventures were probably just as imaginary as those of Conan the Cimmerian.

DS: How do you go about starting a biography?

LSDC: The first thing you do is read everything by or about the man that you can find. Then you hunt down the people who knew him in various ways. The ordinary telephone directory is very useful. Also medical directories and yearbooks of schools and colleges where the person went. You find these people and interview them if you can.

DS: What sort of difficulties did you run into doing the Lovecraft biography?

LSDC: I didn't have any particular difficulties. I had the help of the librarians at Brown University, and a number of Lovecraft's surviving close friends like Frank Belknap Long gave me long interviews and visits in which we talked all about the man, and of course his letters are available in either original or photocopies at Brown, and I got copies of them which they very kindly let me use. And his heir, Mrs. Morrish of Cranston, Rhode Island, gave me permission to quote from the letters, so there was no problem there. Altogether I might say I had a fairly easy time. I made about five visits to Providence and travelled around the country. Some of the professors there showed me around and told me things which were helpful to me. I had a good deal more difficulty with the Howard business because some of the people who know a good deal about him also have the idea that they want to write their biographies or memoirs or whatever. Therefore they don't want to give away any of their precious information. Now whether these works will ever get written is open to question. I know a couple which aren't likely to, considering the age and ability and so forth of the people. But as one of them said, "Well, if I die, it'll die with me." Of course being a damn Yankee didn't help in Texas either. That was where Jane Griffin came in very handy, because we'd take her and she'd open the conversation. She talks Texas and could always say, "Well my grandmother was a such-and-such and she must have been a cousin of yours," and things like that, and then it was old folks at home from there on. But on the other hand I've had to make about three subsequent trips on my own.

DS: How does one get through the legendary persona of the subject to the real person?

LSDC: The question is, what's a real person? How can anybody know what's going on inside the man's mind? You don't unless you shoot him full of some sort of truth drug and question him, and you can't do that, especially with a man who's been dead forty years. You do the best you can. You get all the informtion. For his opinions, you try to find out what he said and wrote on various subjects. For his temperament and personality, you ask the people who knew him and read those who have written about him. Then you figure out as best you can from that. Now, sometimes certain facets of a man's personality come out pretty obviously. For example, if he's always getting into fist fights, why that's pretty significant. You can figure out he's probably paranoid or something. These psychological matters I'd prefer to leave to Jane Griffin, because she knows more about them than I do. If I start sounding off on them, I may say something which is subject to criticism. But, as I say, we do the best we can. If a man like Robert never begins to date a girl until he is 29 years old, you can guess that his sexual orientation is, if not a little askew, at least slow in developing when all the other boys in town are dating them every chance they get. I don't mean that Robert was a homosexual, but he never had been properly socialized, you might say. When he joined the Epworth League about 1930, I guess it was, which is the service club of the Methodist Church, (of which his mother was a member), the reason he did it was because he had an interest in a girl named Ruth Baum, who was the daughter of a prominent family in Cross Plains. But after a few months he got bored and dropped out. He wasn't interested in the religious angle at all. He was interested in Ruth, but when I talked to Ruth about it, she said, "Well we were both pretty shy at the time, and he never said *anything* to me except polite 'Good morning' and things like that." So that's what I mean by not being properly socialized. Partly it was a result of his own temperament and partly a result of his parents' influence, especially that of his mother, who kept him wrapped in cotton wool, you might say, until he was a grown man. Why, he just did not learn how to get along with more than one or two people at a given time. Any larger crowd would make him feel insecure and upset and unhappy.

DS: Does the fact that you discovered Howard's work late and didn't grow up on it give you an advantage of objectivity?

LSDC: It's a little hard to say. Now if I had ever known the man I could doubtless have painted a more detailed picture of his persona than I can by starting on him late. And if I had started earlier, a number of people who either have died or have decided not to hand out any information might have been available as sources. Of course now they are not. His friend David Lee in Cross Plains, for example, died about three years ago. So did Booth Mooney, who was editor of *The Junto*, a little amateur paper that Robert and his literary friends published, and to which he contributed a number of pieces back in the 1920s when he was just getting started as a fiction writer. Booth Mooney went on to become a professional; he was a public relations man who worked for various politicians, and he published about ten books. It was only last summer, I believe, that I tracked him down and found he'd been dead a year and a half.

DS: After the forthcoming Conan novel you mentioned and the biography are done, what further involvement will you have with Howard?

LSDC: I don't foresee any at present. The present contract with Bantam Books calls for six novels. Of those, two have been written by Carter and me; one has been written by Karl Wagner, one by Andrew Offutt, and one is being written by Poul Anderson. I'm to write the remaining one. We don't have any more, and that will mean that if the united Conan series is ever published again, that will make 18 volumes, which is an awful lot of Conan. But I have plenty of other things in mind. I have another fantasy novel, the third of the Jorian trilogy, and I should like to write another Krishna novel, and that book on civilization I talked about, and maybe I'll even try an autobiography. I have, after all, been a lot of interesting places and known a lot of interesting people, even if I myself am not a particularly interesting fellow.

DS: Getting on to writing methods, when you set out to write a novel, how do you begin it?

LSDC: I'm one of these meticulous outliners. Some people sit down and the whole thing pours out. In such a case, it is my belief that the person has usually organized it in his head before it ever appears on paper. I don't work very much that way. I have a general idea, and then gradually fill it out, add more detail, add more complications and the like. For example, I have an idea for a Krishna novel right now. I have a title for it, *The Prisoner of Zhamanak*. That's one of the imaginary places on this pet planet of mine. It begins with a 'Z,' you see, as all the novels in that series have, including the recent *The Hostage of Zir*. And I have a hero for it. He is a character who has appeared in two other stories—Percy Mjipa. He is a black African from Botswana, who is consul for the world federation on this planet, and he is a superior man; that is, he is a tall, lean, frizz-haired black man, quite strong, with a rather rigidly upright character; and also he is, as one of the characters describes him, a bit of an old-fashioned imperialist who thinks that a human being mustn't take any nonsense from these natives. Which is, I think, an entertaining switch.

DS: You mean in the sense of having a black not take nonsense from the natives?

LSDC: Absolutely. That's the sort of thing that happens. You find a lot of people who will take that attitude when they are in a position to do so. The Chinese were certainly the greatest imperialists back in the 12th and 13th Centuries. They sent their great ocean-going junks, which were the world's most advanced ships of the time, all over the Indian Ocean extorting tribute from various Indonesian rajas and people like that.

DS: And the Russians are still at it.

LSDC: Certainly. When politicians find they have the power to do so, they will. After all, the main thing that causes one to become a politician is the desire for power. As Bertrand Russell put it in his Nobel Prize speech, after a man's everyday needs for food, clothing, and shelter are taken care of, why the things that most men go for, their strongest motives, are wealth, power, and glory. And some go more for one and some go for another. If a man is solely concerned with wealth, he becomes a miser. If he is mainly concerned with glory, he will become either a politician or an actor or an explorer. And if he wants power he'll be just a politician, or a corporate executive.

DS: Would you say then that a writer is a mix of wealth and glory?

LSDC: Writers, I think, want the glory mostly. If they didn't, why they'd work at a more conventional job where they could count on a more regular salary. But that's one of the things that has transpired about Robert Howard, and that is that, although he had considerable abilities, he absolutely could not stand any sort of supervision. He couldn't put up with any boss. And so during the period in 1924-27 he held a number of minor jobs, but he never lasted at any of them, and according to him, the job usually ended when he threatened to beat the boss's head off. It wouldn't surprise me but that there was some such incident, from all I've been able to gather about his personality. And that is why he refused to go to college. He had a chance to, but he wouldn't, because he was tired of having to sit in classrooms and take what other people told him, and to be places on time. Later on he regretted the decision, but then it was too late.

DS: Quite a while ago, in the introduction to *The Wheels of If*, you denied that there was any deliberate satirical content to your work. Would you still say this is so?

LSDC: No, I wouldn't say that was so. At that time I thought I was writing purely to amuse, but I can see now that certain satirical elements have a way of sneaking in even when you don't intend them to.

DS: Do you mean simply your observations on the way things work?

LSDC: Yes. You observe how things work and then you figure, why if you just exaggerate a little bit, you could make an entertaining piece out of it.

DS: What about outright didacticism? You had a recent story called "The Figurine," a major sub-theme of which was the more outrageously irrational side of the radical movement of the 1960s—burning down banks to liberate the masses, and all that.

LSDC: Yes, the great youth revolt. Actually I didn't have to exaggerate anything. I have a big file of newspaper clippings under "Education" which deal with the revolt, whole full pages in the *New York Times*. The things that the various characters said are pretty much a paraphrase from what the young people of 1969 and '70 were actually saying, and the sort of thing they were doing. Well, in my case I had the bank saved by a magical rainstorm. But in the case of one bank in California, they burned the whole thing to the ground.

DS: It seemed to me that in this case that perhaps because it was so current, and because you were so strongly opposed that you couldn't get inside the movement to parody it, the humor suffered.

LSDC: That's very possible. But then on the other hand, my hero in those stories, W. Wilson Newbury, is, as you would expect a banker to be, a fairly conservative and slightly stuffy middle-aged character. He says that his banking friends consider him a red-hot liberal, which is entirely possible in such a case. But it reminds me of a New Year's Eve party that I attended on the Main Line over here about 20 years ago, at which I heard one guest telling another, "You know, I *met* a couple of Democrats recently, and they turned out to be quite nice people."

DS: To what exent do you think you can make effective humor out of something which is not by nature humorous—like violence—and is still very current?

LSDC: Of course if you or one of yours gets hurt in the violence, then it ceases to be funny at that point. You have to be pretty careful with that sort of thing. In the case of the story "The Figurine," nobody got killed. They just had a pretty narrow squeak, and if there isn't any actual bloodshed, why humorous things do occur. There are incongruities and absurdities in the real world, and I think it is legitimate to use them. But of course you have to be careful that you don't make fun of or exploit for humor something that your reader takes very seriously, because he won't think it's funny. In fact I dare say that some people who read "The Figurine" who had been sympathetic with the great student revolt didn't find it funny at all. They were outraged at my somewhat irreverent treatment of the whole thing. But then, after all, I have another story coming out called "A Sending of Serpents," which parodies some of the current cults. I won't mention any names, you can figure it out for yourself when the story appears in *F&SF*. But naturally, if you're a true believer in one of those, you're not going to find it funny at all. You're going to be mad as hell.

DS: It also seems to me that the firmest opponent is not in the best position for satire. I think any satire or parody has some degree of sympathy in it. Would you agree?

LSDC: I can't say that I have formulated any firm doctrine, but you may be right.

DS: Do you ever find black humor effective? *Dr. Strangelove*, for example, which is a very humorous movie about blowing up the world.

LSDC: I'm afraid that I feel about *Dr. Strangelove*—I didn't see the movie, but I read enough about it to have an idea—I'm afraid that I react to that somewhat the way a member of one of these cults would react to "A Sending of Serpents," and that is that I'm on the world and blowing it up wouldn't seem the least bit funny to me, I'm afraid.

DS: Do you ever get outraged letters from people about this sort of thing?

LSDC: No, I can't say I really did. Oh, I did hear a couple of remarks on the subject, and I think maybe somebody said something in a fan magazine that indicated he didn't find it very funny. But on the whole I haven't had much trouble of that sort. If you call it trouble. After all, if you don't like the letter you don't have to answer it.

DS: How much crank mail does any established writer get?

LSDC? Let's say I get a fair amount. I took a couple of cracks at Velikovsky and his theories in an article in *Science Digest* back a couple of years ago, and I got a couple of Velikovskians on my neck, a couple of professors in New Jersey, who are professors of sociology and other very soft sciences. The first couple I tried to answer, pointing out the various absurdities, that is the idea that this other planet which is now Venus could have reversed the Earth's rotation by electro-magnetic forces. I pointed out that the magnetic flux on the surface of the Earth is something like one one-hundred-thousandth and one one-millionth of that which you get in an ordinary electric motor, and if you're going to stop something the size of the Earth from spinning in one direction and start it in the other, you're going to have to have a pretty powerful field winding. A lot more than we have on the actual Earth. But all those arguments went right over their heads. All I got was more impassioned, angry letters, so I just dropped the whole matter.

DS: Is this the sort of thing which led you to write the story about cults?

LSDC: Oh, no. I've had an interest in cults for many years. After all, I have written a book called *Spirits, Stars, and Spells; The Profits and Perils of Magic*. I worked on that off and on during the Second World War, when I was in the service. And after the war I wrote it, but I hadn't learned quantitative control, and the thing ballooned up to about a quarter of a million words, and the publisher turned it down, for which I don't blame him. Much later a small publisher got in touch with me through Dick Lupoff, who was their editor at the time, and wanted to know if it could be cut down and used. So I turned that job over to Catherine, and she did a very competent rewrite of it to a reasonable compass, and the thing was duly published. However, it was not then a great commercial success, I may say. That's one of the little lessons that you learn in dealing with cults and pseudo-sciences and such, that if you debunk them, the believers are outraged and the unbelievers don't care. So consequently there is not fortune to be made in debunking. I take a little magazine called *The Skeptical Inquirer*, which is put out by a group of which I am a member of the advisory committee, which tries to debunk Velikovsky and UFOs and Loch Ness monsters and a great many other things of that sort. Well I tell them that they certainly have my best wishes, but I don't think they are going to get very far, because human credulity is unbounded. It always has been.

DS: How about doing a wholesale crankology text?

LSDC: That's what my book is, essentially. It has a chapter on astrology, one on witchcraft, one on theosophy, and so on. I don't have any illusions now that I can convert the world to pure rationality. I'm not sure that would work, even if it could be done.

DS: Thank you, Mr. de Camp.

introducing

a new magazine for the discriminating SF reader who had trouble keeping track of the 1,000+ titles of science fiction and fantasy published during 1978

 Send us a 15¢ stamp and find out why

will save you time and money

- Issued monthly for up-to-date reviews of all new books while still available.

- Comprehensive coverage of American science fiction, fantasy, weird supernatural fiction, nonfiction books about SF, calendars, art books, small press items.

- Selective coverage of British and foreign language first editions.

- Edited by Neil Barron, Author of ANATOMY OF WONDER, the best annotated bibliography of science fiction.

- Published by R. Reginald, Author of SCIENCE FICTION AND FANTASY LITER— ATURE, the standard bibliography of fantastic literature.

- Science fiction and fantasy awards and their winners.

- Obituaries of leading figures and writers in the field.

- Special reports on SF publishing, both here and abroad.

- Review articles on selected writers and movements.

- Retrospective reviews of little-known books that deserve a better fate.

- All issues mailed at first class rates (so you get them next week, and not next month)

Write now for your **FREE** sample copy of issue #1.

SCIENCE FICTION & FANTASY BOOK REVIEW
P.O. Box 2845, San Bernardino, California 92406

(or send us $12 for a charter subscription)